QUICK & EASY
MAKE-AHEAD
MEALS

QUICK & EASY
MAKE-AHEAD
MEALS

Mary Shepherd

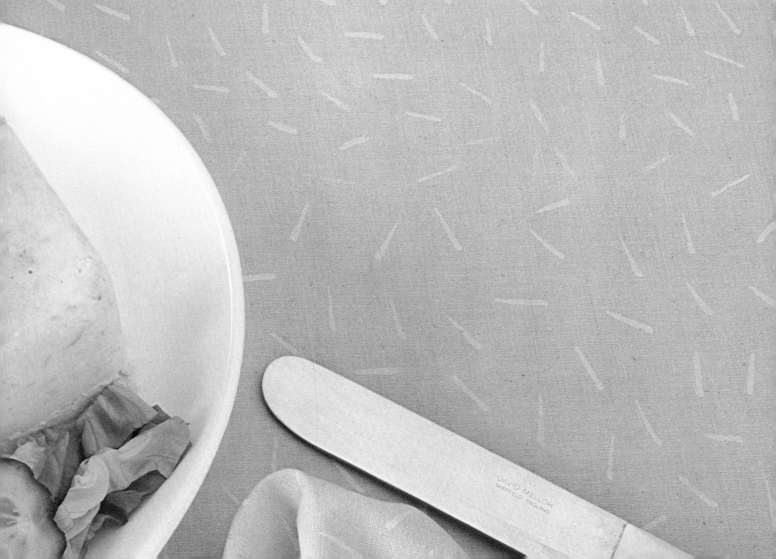

CONTENTS

ANOTHER BEST-SELLING VOLUME FROM HPBooks®

Publisher: Rick Bailey; Editorial Director: Retha M. Davis
Editor: Jeanette P. Egan; Art Director: Don Burton
Book Manufacture: Anthony B. Narducci
Book Assembly: Leslie Sinclair
Typography: Cindy Coatsworth, Michelle Claridge
Recipe testing by International Cookbook Services: Barbara Bloch,
President; Rita Barrett, Director of Testing

Published by HPBooks, Inc.
P.O. Box 5367, Tucson, AZ 85703   602/888-2150
ISBN 0-89586-339-1
Library of Congress Catalog Card Number 84-81923
© 1985 HPBooks, Inc.   Printed in the U.S.A.
1st Printing

Originally published as Cooking for Your Freezer
© 1983 Hennerwood Publications Limited

Cover Photo: Crab-Filled Crepes, page 23

Introduction

Today's busy lifestyle is less hectic if meals are planned and prepared ahead. Prepare dishes for entertaining when you have time to enjoy making them. There are no last-minute surprises; you already know how the dish turned out. Cleanup is also done in advance; this leaves the kitchen clean and tidy for entertaining. Make double batches of favorite recipes; one to serve now, one to freeze for later. Maximize the use of your freezer and refrigerator.

This book contains tested recipes for everything from soup to desserts. All recipes can be made in advance. There are five chapters to provide you with ideas for all occasions. *Soups & Starters* has recipes for light soups and delicious appetizers. Soups are best stored in a concentrated state; this requires less freezer space. Adding milk or cream when heating improves the flavor and texture. *Light Meals & Snacks* is full of ideas for quick meals and snacks that are ready to heat and serve. *Main Dishes* contains recipes for family meals. Imagine serving your family Chili con Carne or Beef Burgundy after a busy day. It's easy if the dish is made ahead. *Special Occasions* has recipes for all your important occasions from anniversaries to entertaining the boss! *Desserts* lets you experiment with exotic ice-cream flavors and elegant cakes. What better way to end a meal than with a dessert from your refrigerator or freezer?

REFRIGERATING PREPARED FOODS

If necessary, cool prepared foods 30 minutes at room temperature. Most soups, appetizers and main dishes can be refrigerated safely one to two days. Baked products can be stored longer. Cover food to prevent loss of moisture and absorption of flavors from other foods. There is a wide variety of containers designed for storing foods. Some containers can go directly from the refrigerator to the microwave oven or regular oven. Others require that the food be transferred to another container before heating. Read labels to determine which type you have.

FREEZING PREPARED FOODS

Freezing is an excellent way of preserving food. But it is essential to use good ingredients, to prepare food correctly and to package and store it carefully. Here are a few reminders of the basic rules.

Cooling—Recipes prepared for freezing should be cooled as quickly as possible after cooking. To cool food quickly, place hot food in its pan in a larger pan or sink containing iced water. Or, pour hot food into a large shallow pan. Cool up to 30 minutes before freezing. Do not leave meat dishes, soups or appetizers at room temperature longer than 30 minutes to prevent bacterial growth and food spoilage.

Open Freezing—Some foods, such as frosted cakes, are difficult to wrap before freezing. Freeze these, unwrapped, on a baking sheet or plate. When frozen, wrap and label. Use the open freezing method for chopped onions, shredded cheese or cookies. After freezing, pack these in plastic freezer bags or rigid freezer containers for storage. Since these are frozen individually, you can remove the amount needed without thawing the entire package.

Seasoning—Lightly season dishes for freezing with salt and pepper. Taste and adjust seasoning immediately before serving. Some flavors change during storage. Garlic, bell peppers, celery and cloves intensify during storage, but the flavor of onion decreases.

Storage—As a rule, use frozen prepared dishes within three months. During this time, there should be no significant change in flavors. However, there are some exceptions to this rule. Store cured meats, fatty fish, leftovers, sandwiches, gelatin dishes, unbaked doughs and highly spiced foods one month or less.

Packaging—Food must be carefully packaged before freezing to prevent changes in flavor and texture. If not properly wrapped, food will lose moisture and become dry and tasteless. Or, food may absorb odors from other foods.

Special freezer paper, heavyweight foil, plastic freezer bags, boilable bags and rigid containers are suitable for freezing food.

Plastic freezer bags are available in several sizes. Do not use regular plastic bags; they are too thin to prevent freezer burn. Always seal bags securely with twist ties.

Rigid plastic containers with tight-fitting lids are

suitable for most foods. Square-shaped containers take less space than round ones.

Foil is malleable and easily formed around awkwardly shaped food. It makes a good barrier for strong flavors, but does tear readily. Use a layer of plastic wrap inside the foil, or put the foil package into a freezer bag. Do not rely on foil alone for anything with sharp bones; pad them first with plastic wrap or waxed paper. Food containing acid, garlic, onion or dried fruit can cause foil to dissolve and discolor food. To prevent this, use a protective wrapping of plastic wrap or waxed paper.

Boilable plastic bags are small pouches that are heat-sealed with a special appliance. If you freeze food on a regular basis, you might want to invest in this equipment. Food frozen in these bags can be dropped into boiling water without thawing. This saves time in cooking and cleanup.

Freezer-to-oven casseroles are suitable for preparing main dishes for freezing. If desired, turn food out after freezing by loosening it with a knife or by quickly dipping the casserole into hot water. Or, line the casserole with foil before cooking the dish. After freezing, lift the foil and food from the casserole; wrap food completely in foil.

Labeling and Storing—It is very important to label food, because once frozen, many foods lose their identity. The label should include the date the food was frozen, recipe name, number of servings and a use-by date. If desired, include the cookbook name and page number or instructions for finishing the dish. For example, a label could say *Make-Ahead Meals, page 14.* Or, *add 1/2 cup milk; heat 20 minutes.* This simplifies cooking and serving.

Keep the freezer well organized. Keep a record of what is frozen and when it should be used to prevent waste. This is also helpful in meal planning.

Thawing—For most recipes, thaw before final cooking or heating, either in the refrigerator or at room temperature. Do not leave casseroles, soups or main dishes at room temperature any longer than is necessary for thawing. If you have a microwave oven, follow the manufacturer's directions for defrosting. Do not use metal or foil containers for heating or thawing in a microwave oven. Many foods can be cooked without thawing. Heat frozen creamed dishes, soups or stews in the top of a double boiler to prevent scorching. Frozen fruits have better texture and flavor if only partially thawed before serving.

Garnishes and Decoration—Garnishes and decorations add interest and color to foods. Add them immediately before serving.

Packaging materials for freezing

Soups & Starters

Chicken Minestrone

4 cups chicken stock
1 ham bone, with some meat
1 medium onion, chopped
2 carrots, thinly sliced
2 celery stalks, thinly sliced
1 cup chopped cooked chicken
4 oz. ziti or other thick macaroni
1/2 cup fresh or frozen green peas
1/2 teaspoon dried leaf oregano or marjoram
Salt
Freshly ground pepper
Grated Parmesan cheese

1. In a large saucepan, combine stock, ham bone, onion, carrots and celery. Bring to a boil. Reduce heat; simmer 20 minutes.
2. Remove ham bone; cut off and chop any meat. Add chopped ham and chicken to soup. Bring to a boil. Cool 30 minutes. Refrigerate overnight, or freeze.
To freeze: Put cooled soup into a rigid freezer container. Cover and label. Freeze up to 1 month. Thaw overnight in refrigerator.
To serve immediately or after refrigerating or thawing: Heat soup in a large saucepan over medium heat. Add remaining ingredients except Parmesan cheese. Simmer 10 minutes or until macaroni is tender. Serve with Parmesan cheese. Makes 4 servings.

Melon & Grape Cup

1-1/2 lb. melon
4 oz. black grapes, halved, seeded
1/4 cup red-grape juice
1/2 cup tonic water

1. Remove and discard seeds from melon; peel. Cut peeled melon into small cubes.
2. In a medium bowl, combine melon cubes, grapes and grape juice. Refrigerate overnight, or freeze.
To freeze: Put into a rigid freezer container. Cover and label. Freeze up to 4 months. Partially thaw frozen mixture before serving.
To serve immediately or after refrigerating or freezing: Spoon into glass dishes; pour tonic water over fruit just before serving. Makes 4 servings.

Beef Stock

2 lb. soup bones
1 onion, chopped
1 celery stalk, chopped
1 carrot, chopped
2 bouquets garni
Salt
Freshly ground pepper
Water

Freeze stock in 2-cup containers. Or, freeze in ice-cube trays; when frozen, pack in plastic freezer bags.
1. Preheat oven to 425F (220C).
2. Put bones into a roasting pan; place in preheated oven. Roast 40 minutes, turning bones over once. Remove from oven.
3. Place browned bones, vegetables and seasonings in a large saucepan. Cover with water. Bring to a boil. Reduce heat; cover. Simmer 2 hours.
4. Strain stock into a large bowl, discarding bones, vegetables and bouquets garni. Refrigerate strained stock until cold. Lift fat from surface. Cover and refrigerate up to 3 days or freeze. Makes about 2 quarts.
To freeze: Pour stock into a rigid freezer container or ice-cube trays. Cover and label. Freeze up to 3 months.
To serve: Use for soups, stews, casseroles or gravy. Cubes may be added, still frozen, to hot soups. Bring to a boil before serving.

Variation
Chicken Stock: Use 2 pounds chicken parts; do not brown. Proceed from Step 3.

Top to bottom: Chicken Minestrone, Melon & Grape Cup

Red-Pepper & Tomato Soup

3 tablespoons butter, melted
1 tablespoon vegetable oil
1 medium onion, chopped
3 small tomatoes, chopped (12 oz.)
2 red bell peppers, chopped
1 tablespoon all-purpose flour
1/4 teaspoon dried leaf basil
Salt
Freshly ground black pepper
2 cups water
1/2 cup half and half or milk

To garnish:
Chopped parsley

---

1. Heat butter and oil in a medium saucepan over medium heat. Add onion; sauté gently until soft. Stir in tomatoes and bell peppers; cook 5 minutes.
2. Stir in flour, basil, salt and pepper. Slowly stir in water. Bring to a boil, stirring constantly. Reduce heat; cover. Simmer 30 minutes, stirring frequently.
3. In a blender or food processor fitted with a steel blade, process soup until pureed. Rub puree through a sieve. Refrigerate overnight, or freeze.
To freeze: Pour into a rigid freezer container. Cover and label. Freeze up to 2 months. To serve frozen soup, thaw overnight in refrigerator. Finish soup as directed below.
To serve immediately or after refrigerating or thawing: Place pureed soup in a medium saucepan over medium heat. Bring to a boil, stirring occasionally. Add cream or milk; heat, but do not boil. Season to taste. Garnish with chopped parsley. Makes 4 servings.

Creamy Cabbage Soup

1/4 cup butter
3 cups finely shredded cabbage
3/4 cup chicken stock
1-1/4 cups milk
Salt
White pepper

To garnish:
Chopped chives or green-onion tops

This basic soup is delicious. Any cooked vegetables, such as sliced button mushrooms, chopped asparagus tips, peas, carrots, and corn, or chopped cooked ham can be added. Make double or triple the amount to freeze.

1. Melt butter in a medium saucepan over low heat. Add cabbage. Cover; cook about 30 minutes or until cabbage is soft, stirring occasionally.
2. Add stock to cooked cabbage. In a blender or food processor fitted with a steel blade, process cabbage and stock in batches until smooth. Cool 30 minutes. Refrigerate overnight, or freeze.
To freeze: Pour into a rigid freezer container. Cover and label. Freeze up to 1 month. Thaw frozen cabbage mixture overnight in refrigerator.
To serve immediately or after refrigerating or thawing: Place cabbage mixture in a saucepan; bring to a boil, stirring occasionally. Add milk; season with salt and pepper. Garnish with chopped chives or onion tops. Makes 4 servings.

Left to right: Creamy Cabbage Soup, Red-Pepper & Tomato Soup, Whole-Wheat Soda Bread

Whole-Wheat Soda Bread

1-1/2 cups whole-wheat flour
1-1/2 cups all-purpose flour
1 tablespoon sugar
1 teaspoon salt
1 teaspoon baking soda
1/4 cup butter or margarine
1 tablespoon white vinegar
1 cup milk

1. Preheat oven to 375F (190C). Grease a round 8-inch baking pan; set aside.
2. In a medium bowl, combine flours, sugar, salt and baking soda. Using 2 knives or a pastry blender, cut in butter or margarine until mixture resembles coarse crumbs. Stir vinegar into milk; add to flour mixture, stirring to make a soft dough.
3. Turn out dough onto a lightly floured surface; knead 8 to 10 times or until smooth. Shape into a round flat loaf. Place dough in prepared pan; cut a deep cross on top of bread.
4. Bake in preheated oven 45 to 50 minutes or until golden brown. Remove from pan. Cool completely on a wire rack.
To freeze: Wrap cooled bread in foil; label. Freeze up to 3 months. Thaw frozen bread at room temperature 1-1/2 to 2 hours.
To serve immediately or after thawing: Serve cold or heat in a 350F (175C) oven. Makes 1 loaf.

Bacon & Liver Pâté

4 bacon slices, chopped
8 oz. turkey or chicken livers, chopped
1 hard-cooked egg
1 garlic clove, crushed
2 tablespoons brandy
1 tablespoon whipping cream
1/4 teaspoon dried leaf thyme
Pinch of ground mace
Salt
Freshly ground pepper

To garnish:
2 hard-cooked eggs, separated
Parsley sprigs

1. Place bacon in a large skillet over medium heat. Sauté until almost done. Add livers; cook 10 minutes, stirring occasionally.
2. In a blender or food processor fitted with a steel blade, combine cooked bacon-and-liver mixture and remaining ingredients except for garnish. Process until smooth. Spoon into 4 ramekin dishes. Refrigerate, or freeze.
To freeze: Cover and label. Freeze up to 1 month. Allow to thaw in refrigerator 6 to 8 hours.
To serve after refrigerating or thawing: To make the garnish, with a knife, finely chop egg whites; press egg yolks through a sieve. Arrange chopped egg whites and sieved yolks in rings on top of pâté with a parsley sprig in center. Serve with hot toast. Makes 4 servings.

Clockwise from left: Blue-Cheese Soufflés, Country Chicken Pâté, Bacon & Liver Pâté

Country Chicken Pâté

1 cup minced cooked chicken
1/4 cup minced cooked ham
1 teaspoon grated lemon peel
2 teaspoons chopped fresh parsley
1/4 teaspoon dried leaf tarragon
Salt
Freshly ground pepper
1/2 cup butter, melted

To garnish:
Lettuce leaves
Tomato slices
Parsley or tarragon sprigs

1. In a medium bowl, combine all ingredients except garnish.
2. Press chicken mixture into 4 individual ramekin dishes or foil-lined custard cups.
3. Chill until mixture is firm. Refrigerate overnight, or freeze.

To freeze: Wrap and label. Freeze up to 1 month. Thaw in refrigerator about 6 hours before serving.

To serve after refrigerating or thawing: Turn out onto plates lined with lettuce leaves and tomato slices. Garnish with a parsley or tarragon sprig. Serve with Melba toast. Makes 4 servings.

Variation
Potted Shrimps: Substitute 8 ounces minced cooked shrimp for chicken and ham. Substitute a pinch of red (cayenne) pepper for tarragon. Substitute lemon wedges for tomato slices.

Blue-Cheese Soufflés

1/4 cup butter or margarine
1/2 cup all-purpose flour
1-1/2 cups milk
3 eggs, separated
2/3 cup fresh bread crumbs
1/2 teaspoon dry mustard
White pepper
1 cup crumbled blue cheese

1. Heavily grease 6 (2/3-cup, 3-1/2-inch-diameter) freezer-to-oven ramekins.
2. Melt butter or margarine in a medium saucepan over medium heat. Stir in flour; cook 1 minute, stirring constantly. Gradually stir in milk; boil until sauce is thickened, stirring constantly. Cool slightly.
3. Beat in egg yolks, bread crumbs, mustard and white pepper until blended. Add blue cheese; stir until cheese is melted. Pour cheese mixture into a large bowl.
4. In another large bowl, beat egg whites until stiff peaks form. Fold beaten egg whites into cheese mixture. Divide mixture evenly among greased ramekins. Freeze.

To freeze: Place filled ramekins on a baking sheet. Open freeze. Wrap each frozen soufflé with foil; label. Freeze up to 1 month.

To serve after freezing: Preheat oven to 425F (220C). Unwrap; place frozen soufflés in preheated oven. Bake 35 to 40 minutes or until raised and golden brown on top. Serve immediately; this soufflé will not wait. Makes 6 servings.

Smoked-Salmon Boats

1-1/4 cups all-purpose flour
1/2 teaspoon salt
7 tablespoons shortening
3 tablespoons iced water
Filling:
1/3 lb. smoked-salmon trimmings, finely chopped
1 tablespoon lemon juice
1/4 teaspoon dried dill weed
1 tablespoon mayonnaise
1/4 cup whipping cream, lightly whipped
Salt
Freshly ground pepper

To garnish:
Paprika
Fresh dill sprigs

1. Preheat oven to 400F (205C).
2. To make pastry, in a medium bowl, combine flour and salt. Using a pastry blender or 2 knives, cut in shortening until mixture resembles fine bread crumbs. Add water; toss with a fork until dough begins to hold together. Press dough into a ball.
3. Roll out dough on a lightly floured surface. Use to line 8 boat-shaped tart pans. With a fork, prick well; place on a baking sheet. Bake in preheated oven 15 minutes or until golden brown. Cool in pans 10 minutes. Remove from pans; cool completely on a wire rack.
4. To make filling, in a medium bowl, combine all filling ingredients. Refrigerate overnight, or freeze.
To freeze: Spoon filling into a rigid freezer container. Cover and label. Freeze up to 1 month. Pack pastry boats separately in a rigid freezer container. Cover and label. Freeze up to 3 months. Thaw frozen filling in refrigerator about 6 hours. Thaw pastry boats at room temperature 30 minutes.
To serve after refrigerating or thawing: Stir filling; spoon into baked pastry boats. Sprinkle with paprika; garnish with fresh dill. Makes 8 pastries.

Easy Cheese Ball

2 cups shredded Cheddar cheese (8 oz.)
1 (3-oz.) pkg. cream cheese, room temperature
2 oz. crumbled blue cheese, room temperature (1/2 cup)
1 garlic clove, crushed
1/2 teaspoon Worcestershire sauce

1. In a blender or food processor fitted with a steel blade, blend Cheddar cheese, cream cheese, blue cheese, garlic and Worcestershire sauce until smooth.
2. Shape cheese mixture into a ball. Wrap in plastic wrap or waxed paper. Refrigerate 2 to 3 days, or freeze.
To freeze: Cover wrapped ball with foil; label. Freeze up to 1 month. Thaw wrapped cheese ball in refrigerator overnight.
To serve after refrigerating or thawing: Unwrap cheese ball. Place on a serving plate. Serve with crackers. Makes 6 to 8 servings.

Variations
Roll cheese ball in chopped nuts before wrapping. Or, roll in chopped parsley immediately before serving.

Chicken-Liver Pâté

1 lb. chicken livers
1/4 cup rendered chicken fat, butter or margarine
1 onion, finely chopped
1 garlic clove, minced
2 tablespoons Marsala or sweet sherry
Salt
Freshly ground pepper
2 hard-cooked eggs, chopped

To garnish:
Chopped fresh parsley
Assorted crackers or cocktail bread

1. Lightly grease a 2-1/2-cup mold with butter or margarine; set aside.
2. Trim chicken livers; cut in half. Rinse liver halves under cold running water; pat dry with paper towels.
3. Melt chicken fat, butter or margarine in a medium skillet over medium heat. Add onion; sauté until transparent. Add garlic and chicken livers; sauté 5 minutes or until livers are no longer pink.
4. In a blender or food processor fitted with a steel blade, process liver mixture until almost smooth. Add Marsala or sherry, salt and pepper; process 1 minute. Add eggs; process 1 minute.
5. Spoon into prepared mold; smooth top.
To refrigerate: Cover and refrigerate until thoroughly chilled. Refrigerate up to 2 days.
To serve after refrigerating: Unmold onto a serving plate; garnish with chopped parsley. Serve with crackers or cocktail bread. Makes 8 servings.

Left to right: Gazpacho Ice, Smoked-Salmon Boats

Gazpacho Ice

1 medium tomato, diced
1 medium cucumber, peeled, diced
1 small green bell pepper, diced
1 small onion, diced
1 garlic clove, crushed
1 to 2 tablespoons red-wine vinegar
1 teaspoon paprika
1/2 (8-oz.) pkg. cream cheese, room temperature
1/2 cup whipping cream
1 (1/4-oz.) envelope unflavored gelatin (1 tablespoon)
1/4 cup water
Salt
Freshly ground black pepper
Hot-pepper sauce

To garnish:
Lettuce leaves
Chopped green olives

1. In a blender or food processor fitted with a steel blade, process tomato, cucumber, green pepper, onion and garlic until pureed. Stir in vinegar and paprika. Press pureed mixture through a sieve into a large bowl; set aside.
2. Without rinsing blender or food processor, process cream cheese and cream until smooth. Add pureed vegetable mixture, 1/2 cup at a time; process until blended.
3. In a small saucepan, combine gelatin and water. Stir well; let stand 3 minutes. Stir over low heat until gelatin dissolves; set aside to cool. Stir cooled gelatin into puree. Season with salt, pepper and hot-pepper sauce.
To freeze: Pour into a 4-cup rigid freezer container; cover and label. Freeze 5 to 6 hours or until thoroughly frozen. Store up to 1 month.
To serve after freezing: Place in refrigerator several hours, or let stand at room temperature to soften slightly before serving. Spoon into individual serving bowls. Place bowls on lettuce-lined plates; garnish with chopped olives. Makes 6 to 8 servings.

Light Meals & Snacks

Stuffed Peppers

4 large green bell peppers
1 tablespoon vegetable oil
1 large onion, chopped
4 oz. button mushrooms, sliced
1/4 cup chopped almonds or pecans
1/3 cup dried apricots, soaked overnight,
    drained, chopped
1 cup cooked long-grain white rice
1 egg, slightly beaten
Worcestershire sauce
Salt
Freshly ground black pepper

Sauce:
2 tablespoons butter or margarine
2 tablespoons all-purpose flour
1 cup milk
1 teaspoon prepared brown mustard
1 cup shredded Cheddar cheese (4 oz.)
Salt
Freshly ground pepper

1. Cut off stem end of each bell pepper. Remove and discard seeds and inner pith. If peppers do not stand straight, trim to level bottoms.
2. Heat oil in a large skillet over medium heat. Add onion; sauté 5 minutes or until onion is softened.
3. Add mushrooms, nuts and apricots; cook 3 minutes. Stir in rice and egg. Season with Worcestershire sauce, salt and pepper.
4. Fill bell peppers with rice mixture; stand filled peppers upright in a baking dish large enough to hold them in a single layer.
5. To make sauce, melt butter or margarine in a medium saucepan. Stir in flour; cook 1 minute, stirring constantly. Gradually stir in milk. Bring to a boil; cook until smooth and thickened, stirring constantly. Stir in mustard and half of cheese. Season with salt and pepper. Pour sauce around filled peppers. Sprinkle filled peppers with remaining cheese. Cool; refrigerate overnight, or freeze.
To freeze: Cover and label. Freeze up to 3 months. Thaw in refrigerator overnight before baking.
To serve immediately or after refrigerating or thawing: Cover with foil. Bake in a preheated 350F (175C) oven about 1 hour or until peppers are tender. Makes 4 servings.

Variation
Fill bell peppers with freshly made Savory Hamburger Mix, page 28. Pipe mashed potatoes on top. Substitute a tomato sauce for cheese sauce. Freeze and cook as above.

Pizza Omelet

2 tablespoons vegetable oil
1 small onion, finely chopped
1-1/2 cups diced, peeled, parboiled potatoes (8 oz.)
1/2 green bell pepper, diced
1 large tomato, peeled, seeded, chopped
6 pimento-stuffed green olives, chopped
6 eggs
Salt
Freshly ground black pepper

To serve:
1 tablespoon vegetable oil
1 tablespoon butter
3/4 cup shredded sharp Cheddar cheese (3 oz.)
4 anchovy fillets, halved lengthwise
4 pimento-stuffed green olives, halved

Spanish Omelet, full of interesting vegetables and flavors, makes a super snack. Here it is used as a base for a cheese topping that makes it into a meal. Eat the plain omelet, cold, cut into small wedges as a cocktail snack.

1. Heat oil in a 9-inch, non-stick, flameproof skillet. Add onion; sauté gently until softened. Add potatoes, bell pepper, tomato and chopped olives; cook 5 minutes, stirring gently.
2. In a medium bowl, beat eggs; season with salt and pepper. Pour egg mixture over vegetable mixture in skillet. Cook about 5 minutes or until eggs are set on bottom.
3. Put skillet under a preheated broiler. Cook until top is set and lightly browned. With a spatula, loosen omelet from pan. Turn out omelet onto a waxed-paper-covered wire rack. Cool. Refrigerate overnight, or freeze.

To freeze: Open freeze omelet on a baking sheet. When frozen, wrap with foil; label. Freeze up to 1 month. Thaw in refrigerator 4 to 6 hours.

To serve immediately or after refrigerating or thawing: Heat oil and butter in a 9-inch flameproof skillet over medium-low heat. Place omelet in skillet; heat 15 minutes, shaking pan occasionally. Preheat broiler. Top warm omelet with cheese; put under preheated broiler until cheese is melted. Garnish with anchovy strips and olives. Serve immediately with hot garlic bread and a salad. Makes 4 servings.

Top to bottom: Stuffed Peppers, Pizza Omelet

Many school children and workers take packed lunches every day. Sandwiches are convenient for packing and eating. But sandwiches take time to make. Freezer sandwiches are ideal. They can be made any time and then frozen. Placed directly into a lunch box, frozen sandwiches will be thawed and fresh at lunch time. If desired, freeze only the fillings; make sandwiches as needed.

Most traditional fillings can be used. However, hard-cooked eggs and mayonnaise do not freeze well. Hard-cooked egg whites become rubbery when frozen; mayonnaise separates. Here are two rather unusual fillings.

Curried-Beef & Banana Sandwiches

12 oz. corned beef, minced
1-1/2 teaspoons prepared brown mustard
1/2 cup banana-flavored or plain yogurt
1/4 teaspoon curry powder
Salt
Butter, room temperature
20 bread slices

1. In a medium bowl, combine corned beef, mustard, yogurt, curry powder and salt. Butter bread.
2. Spread filling over 1/2 of buttered bread slices; top with remaining bread slices.
To freeze: Wrap sandwiches individually in foil or freezer paper; label. Freeze up to 1 month. Thaw in refrigerator or pack frozen for lunch. Makes 10 sandwiches.

Smoked-Fish Sandwiches

12 oz. kippers or other smoked fish, minced
Grated peel and juice of 1 lemon
1 small apple, peeled, minced
Salt
Freshly ground pepper
Butter, room temperature
20 whole-wheat-bread slices

1. In a medium bowl, combine kippers or other smoked fish, lemon peel, lemon juice and apple. Season to taste with salt and pepper.
2. Lightly butter bread; spread 1/2 of buttered bread slices with filling. Top with remaining bread slices.
To freeze: Wrap sandwiches individually in foil or freezer paper; label. Freeze up to 1 month. Thaw in refrigerator or pack frozen for lunch. Makes 10 sandwiches.

Family Sandwich

Egg Filling:
2 tablespoons butter or margarine
3 eggs
2 tablespoons milk
Salt
Freshly ground pepper
3 green onions, finely chopped

Chicken Filling:
3/4 cup minced cooked chicken
1 celery stalk, thinly sliced
1/4 teaspoon curry powder
2 to 3 tablespoons mayonnaise-style salad dressing

Cheese Filling:
1 cup finely shredded Cheddar cheese (4 oz.)
2 tomatoes, peeled, finely chopped
1 tablespoon mayonnaise-style salad dressing
1 (7-inch) round loaf whole-wheat bread
Butter, room temperature

To garnish:
Lettuce leaves

This is a good way to use up leftover meat or cheese. Take the filled loaf on a picnic or eat for a light lunch or supper at home. Fillings can be varied according to your needs.

1. To make egg filling, melt butter or margarine in a medium skillet over medium heat. In a medium bowl, beat eggs with a whisk; beat in milk, salt and pepper until blended. Add egg mixture to skillet; cook until scrambled, stirring constantly. Stir in onions; cool.
2. To make chicken filling, in a medium bowl, combine chicken, celery and curry powder. Add salad dressing until of spreading consistency.
3. To make cheese filling, in a medium bowl, combine cheese, tomatoes and salad dressing.
4. Slice loaf horizontally into 4 layers. Spread each cut surface with butter. Spread each filling over 1 layer. Reassemble loaf.

To freeze: Wrap filled loaf in foil; label. Freeze up to 1 month. Thaw in refrigerator 6 hours or overnight.

To serve immediately or after thawing: Slice filled loaf vertically. Serve with lettuce leaves. Makes 4 to 6 servings.

Lamb Pita Pockets

Marinade:
2 tablespoons vegetable oil
2 tablespoons red wine
1/4 teaspoon chili powder
1/4 teaspoon ground coriander
1 bouquet garni
Salt
Freshly ground pepper
12 oz. lean lamb, cut in thin slices
1 medium onion, thinly sliced
2 teaspoons sesame seeds

To serve:
4 pita breads
Shredded Chinese cabbage or lettuce
Tomato slices
Cucumber slices

1. To make marinade, in a large bowl, combine oil, wine, chili powder, coriander, bouquet garni, salt and pepper. Add lamb, onion and sesame seeds; stir well. Cover and refrigerate 4 hours or overnight, stirring occasionally.

2. Transfer lamb and marinade to a saucepan over medium heat. Cook gently 25 to 30 minutes or until lamb and onion are tender. Add a little water, if necessary. Discard bouquet garni. Cool 30 minutes. Refrigerate overnight, or freeze.

To freeze: Spoon cooled meat mixture into a rigid freezer container. Cover and label. Freeze up to 3 months. Thaw overnight in refrigerator.

To serve after refrigerating or thawing: Spoon meat mixture into a medium saucepan. Cook over medium heat 25 to 30 minutes or until hot. Make a short cut along edge of pita breads; open to make pockets. Fill with hot meat mixture. Add Chinese cabbage or lettuce, tomato and cucumber to each sandwich. Serve warm. Makes 4 sandwiches.

Left to right: Family Sandwich, Lamb Pita Pockets

Homemade Buns

1 (1/4-oz.) pkg. active dry yeast (1 tablespoon)
1 teaspoon sugar
1/2 cup warm water (110F, 45C)
1/4 cup vegetable shortening
2 teaspoons salt
1/2 cup milk, scalded
About 3-1/4 cups all-purpose flour

1. In a large bowl, combine yeast, sugar and water. Stir until dissolved. Let stand 5 to 10 minutes or until foamy.
2. Add shortening and salt to hot milk, stirring until melted. Cool to lukewarm.
3. Stir cooled milk mixture into yeast mixture. Stir in 2-1/2 to 3 cups flour or enough flour to make a soft dough.
4. Turn out dough on a lightly floured surface; knead in enough remaining flour to make a stiff dough. Knead until dough is smooth and elastic, 8 to 10 minutes.
5. Clean and grease bowl. Place dough in greased bowl; turn to coat. Cover with a clean towel. Let rise in a warm place, free from drafts, until doubled in bulk, 1 to 1-1/2 hours. Grease 2 baking sheets.
6. Punch down dough. Cut dough into 8 equal pieces. Shape each piece into a ball. Flatten each ball with palm of your hand into a round bun 4 inches in diameter. Place buns on greased baking sheets. Cover; let rise 25 minutes or until doubled in bulk.
7. Preheat oven to 425F (220C). Dust buns lightly with flour. Bake in preheated oven 12 to 15 minutes or until golden brown. Remove from baking sheets; cool completely on wire racks.
To freeze: Place cooled buns in plastic freezer bags. Seal and label. Freeze up to 6 months. Thaw at room temperature 1 hour.
To serve after thawing: Wrap in foil; heat in preheated 350F (175C) oven 8 to 10 minutes. Makes 8 buns.

Variations

Quick Supper Pizzas: Slice buns in half. Toast lightly; spread with butter. Top with smoked sausages slices and tomato slices. Sprinkle with shredded Cheddar cheese; place under a preheated broiler until cheese is melted and lightly browned. Serve hot.

This recipe can also be used to make 12 small rolls. Serve rolls warm for breakfast, or split and fill like pita pockets.

1/Stir in enough flour to make a soft dough.

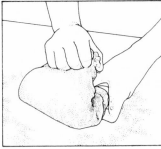

2/Knead dough on a floured surface.

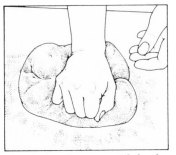

3/Push dough away with heel of your hand.

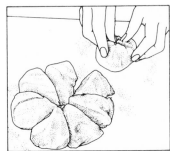

4/Cut dough into 8 pieces. Shape into balls.

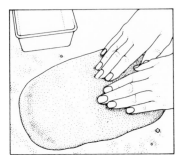

1/Shape dough into a rectangle as wide as your loaf pan is long.

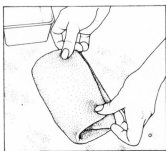

2/Fold dough into thirds to fit loaf pan. Press edges to seal.

Whole-Wheat Bread

2 (1/4-oz.) pkgs. active dry yeast (2 tablespoons)
1 tablespoon granulated sugar
1/4 cup warm water (110F, 45C)
1/3 cup butter or margarine
1/3 cup molasses
1/4 cup packed dark-brown sugar
1 tablespoon salt
2-1/4 cups milk, scalded
3-1/2 cups whole-wheat flour
4 cups all-purpose flour
Sesame seeds or poppy seeds

Double recipe, if desired.

1. In a large bowl, combine yeast, granulated sugar and water. Stir until dissolved. Let stand 5 to 10 minutes or until foamy.
2. Add butter or margarine, molasses, brown sugar and salt to hot milk, stirring until blended. Cool to lukewarm.
3. Stir cooled milk mixture into yeast. Beat in 2 cups whole-wheat flour and 2 cups all-purpose flour. Stir in remaining whole-wheat flour and 1-1/2 cups all-purpose flour or enough remaining all-purpose flour to make a soft dough.
4. Turn out dough onto a lightly floured surface; knead in enough remaining all-purpose flour to make a stiff dough. Knead until smooth and elastic, 8 to 10 minutes.
5. Clean and grease bowl. Place dough in greased bowl; turn to coat. Cover with a clean towel. Let rise in a warm place, free from drafts, until doubled in bulk. Grease 2 (9" x 5") loaf pans; set aside.
6. Punch down dough. Divide dough in half. Shape each half into a loaf; place in prepared pans. Cover; let rise until doubled.
7. Preheat oven to 375F (190C). Brush tops of loaves with water; sprinkle with sesame or poppy seeds. Bake 35 to 40 minutes or until browned. Remove from pans. Cool on a wire rack.
To freeze: Wrap cooled bread in foil; place in a plastic freezer bag. Seal and label. Freeze up to 6 months. Thaw wrapped bread at room temperature 2 to 3 hours.
To serve after thawing: Heat in a preheated 300F (150C) oven 15 to 20 minutes or until warm, if desired. Makes 2 loaves.

Top to bottom: Whole-Wheat Bread, Homemade Buns, Quick Supper Pizzas

Chicken Chowder

4 bacon slices, chopped
1 onion, finely chopped
2 celery stalks, sliced
1-1/2 cups diced potatoes
1/2 cup whole-kernel corn
1-1/2 cups chicken stock
1 cup diced cooked chicken or turkey
Salt
Freshly ground pepper
Pinch ground mace
1/2 cup half and half

Chowder is an American word thought to come from the name of the cooking pot that fishermen used to throw their catch into when they returned safely from the sea. The community shared in celebrating their homecoming. The thick soup/stew was a particular feature of New England cooking. Today, many ingredients other than fish are used to make chowder. Double recipe, if desired.

1. Place bacon in a large saucepan over medium heat. Sauté until partially cooked. Add onion; sauté 5 minutes or until softened.
2. Add celery, potatoes, corn and stock. Bring to a boil; reduce heat. Cover; simmer 15 minutes.
3. Add chicken or turkey; cook 5 minutes longer. Season with salt, pepper and mace. Cool 30 minutes.
To freeze: Pour cooled chowder into a rigid freezer container. Cover and label. Freeze up to 1 month. Thaw overnight in refrigerator.
To serve immediately or after refrigerating or thawing: Place chowder in a saucepan over medium heat. Bring to a boil, stirring occasionally. Simmer 5 minutes. Stir in half and half; heat but do not boil. Adjust seasoning, if necessary. Serve with warm Whole-Wheat Soda Bread, page 11, and butter. Makes 4 servings.

Clockwise from upper left: Sunday-Night Pea Soup, Crab-Filled Crepes, Chicken Chowder

Crepes

2 cups all-purpose flour
1/4 teaspoon salt
4 eggs
2 cups milk
1/4 cup butter or margarine, melted
Butter or margarine

1. In a large bowl, combine flour and salt. In a medium bowl, with a whisk, beat eggs; beat in milk until combined. Slowly pour egg mixture into flour, beating constantly. Beat until mixture is blended and batter is smooth. Slowly add melted butter or margarine, beating until combined.
2. Or, place ingredients in a blender or food processor. Process 1 to 2 minutes or until batter is smooth.
3. Pour batter into a pitcher. Cover and refrigerate at least 1 hour.
4. Stir refrigerated batter. If batter has thickened slightly, stir in a few teaspoons of milk.
5. Melt 1 teaspoon butter or margarine in a 6- or 7-inch skillet or crepe pan over medium heat. Pour in 3 tablespoons batter or enough to make a thin layer in bottom of pan. Cook over medium heat 1-1/2 minutes or until small bubbles begin to form on crepe's surface. With a spatula, turn crepe over; cook 1-1/2 minutes. Remove cooked crepe to a flat plate; repeat with remaining batter. Add more butter or margarine to skillet or pan as necessary. Cool. Refrigerate up to 2 days or freeze.
To freeze: Place waxed paper between each crepe. Wrap stacked crepes in freezer wrap or foil. Label. Freeze up to 2 months. Thaw at room temperature until crepes are soft and pliable.
To serve immediately or after refrigerating or thawing: When ready to use, remove only as many crepes as needed. Fill and heat. Makes about 34 crepes.

Crab-Filled Crepes

Crabmeat Filling:
1 (6-1/2-oz.) can crabmeat, drained
2 tablespoons butter or margarine
2 tablespoons all-purpose flour
1 cup milk
1/2 cup shredded Swiss cheese (2 oz.)
1/4 cup dry vermouth or dry white wine
2 hard-cooked eggs, chopped
Salt
Freshly ground pepper
8 crepes
2 to 3 tablespoons half and half
1/2 cup dairy sour cream

If desired, refrigerate crabmeat filling overnight. Do not freeze.

1. Pick over crabmeat; set aside.
2. Melt butter or margarine in a medium saucepan over medium heat. Stir in flour; cook 1 minute, stirring constantly. Slowly stir in milk; cook until slightly thickened, stirring constantly. Add cheese; stir over low heat until cheese is melted. Remove from heat; stir in vermouth or wine, crabmeat, eggs, salt and pepper.
3. Preheat oven to 350F (175C). Butter an 11" x 7" baking dish; set aside.
4. Spoon 1-1/2 tablespoons crabmeat mixture onto each crepe. Fold crepe over filling; place, seam side down, in buttered baking dish. Cover; bake 15 to 20 minutes or until heated through.
5. Stir 1 to 2 tablespoons half and half into sour cream. Place crepes on a serving dish; spoon sour-cream mixture across center. Makes 8 filled crepes.

Sunday-Night Pea Soup

6 oz. dried peas
2 oz. dried lentils
About 6 cups water
1-1/2 lb. smoked ham hock
1 large onion, chopped
2 bay leaves
Freshly ground pepper

This is a substantial soup. Serve as a main dish. Double recipe, if desired.

1. Put peas and lentils in a large saucepan. Cover with cold water; let stand 12 hours.
2. Drain off and discard soaking water. Add ham, onion, bay leaves and pepper. Add enough water to cover.
3. Bring to a boil. Reduce heat; cover. Simmer 2 hours or until peas are tender.
4. Lift out ham. Remove skin and meat from bone; discard bone and skin. Cut meat into chunks; set aside.
5. In a blender or food processor fitted with a steel blade, process soup, in batches, until smooth. Process soup twice, if necessary. Add ham chunks to puree. Cool 30 minutes.
To freeze: Pour cooled soup into 2 (4-cup) rigid freezer containers. Cover and label. Freeze up to 2 months. Thaw in refrigerator overnight or thaw while heating.
To serve after refrigerating or freezing: Heat soup in a large saucepan over medium heat. Bring to a boil, stirring occasionally. Taste; adjust seasoning, if necessary. Add a little milk if soup is too thick. Serve with whole-wheat rolls or toast. Makes 8 servings.

Cannelloni with Tomato Sauce

Sauce:
2 (15-oz.) cans tomatoes, chopped
1 onion, finely chopped
2 tablespoons tomato paste
1 teaspoon Italian seasoning
1 red bell pepper, finely chopped
1/2 cup red wine
1/2 cup chicken stock
2 teaspoons red-currant jelly
Salt
Freshly ground black pepper

Filling:
1 (10-oz.) pkg. frozen chopped spinach, cooked, drained
1/2 cup cottage cheese
2 tablespoons dry bread crumbs
Freshly grated nutmeg
8 cannelloni tubes
Grated Parmesan cheese

Filling cooked cannelloni tubes can be quite difficult. In this recipe, uncooked pasta is filled. Sauce is made thinner than usual; extra liquid is absorbed by pasta during cooking. If desired, pasta can be precooked, following directions on package. Use slightly less liquid in sauce. Double recipe, if desired.

1. To make sauce, in a large saucepan over medium heat, combine all sauce ingredients. Bring to a boil. Reduce heat; cover. Simmer 20 minutes, stirring occasionally. Cool 30 minutes.
2. To make filling, in a medium bowl, combine spinach, cottage cheese, bread crumbs and nutmeg. Spoon filling into uncooked cannelloni tubes.
3. Spread half of sauce in a shallow freezer-to-oven dish, large enough to hold cannelloni without touching. Arrange stuffed cannelloni in a single layer, not touching and with sauce under and between them.
4. Cover completely with remaining sauce. Cool 30 minutes. Refrigerate overnight, or freeze.
To freeze: Cover with waxed paper and foil or a lid; label. Freeze up to 3 months. Do not thaw before baking.
To serve after refrigerating or freezing: Bake frozen cannelloni in a preheated 375F (190C) oven 1-1/4 hours or until cannelloni are tender and sauce is bubbling. If refrigerated, bake about 40 minutes. Sprinkle with Parmesan cheese. Serve extra cheese in a separate dish. Makes 4 servings.

Spaghetti Layer Bake

2 tablespoons vegetable oil
1 large onion, chopped
1 lb. tomatoes, peeled, chopped
4 oz. mushrooms, chopped
1 tablespoon tomato paste
1 teaspoon dried leaf oregano
Salt
Freshly ground pepper
8 oz. ground beef or pork
1 garlic clove, crushed
6 oz. spaghetti

Topping:
2 tablespoons butter
2 tablespoons all-purpose flour
1 cup milk
1 egg, slightly beaten
1 teaspoon dry mustard
3/4 cup shredded sharp Cheddar cheese (3 oz.)

---

1. Heat 1 tablespoon oil in a large saucepan over medium heat. Add onion; sauté until soft. Add tomatoes, mushrooms, tomato paste, oregano, salt and pepper. Cook 5 minutes.
2. To make meatballs, in a medium bowl, combine meat, garlic, salt and pepper. With floured hands, shape mixture into 16 meatballs.
3. Heat remaining oil in a large skillet over medium heat. Add meatballs; sauté until lightly browned on all sides. As meatballs brown, remove from skillet; drain on paper towels.
4. Cook spaghetti according to package directions until barely tender. Drain cooked spaghetti; add to tomato mixture.
5. Place 1/2 of spaghetti mixture into a deep 1-1/2-quart freezer-to-oven dish. Top with meatballs; cover with remaining spaghetti mixture.
6. To make topping, melt butter in a saucepan over medium heat. Stir in flour; cook 1 minute, stirring constantly. Gradually stir in milk. Bring to a boil, stirring constantly; cook until thickened and smooth. Cool slightly. Beat in egg, mustard and cheese. Stir until blended and cheese is melted. Season with salt and pepper.
7. Pour topping over spaghetti. Cool 30 minutes. Refrigerate overnight, or freeze.
To freeze: Cover and label. Freeze up to 1 month. Thaw in refrigerator overnight.
To serve immediately or after refrigerating or thawing: Remove cover; bake in a preheated 375F (190C) oven 1 to 1-1/4 hours or until hot and bubbling. Topping should be set and browned. Serve with a green salad or vegetables. Makes 4 servings.

Meat Loaf

1 cup minced cooked roast beef or lamb
1/2 cup minced cooked ham
1 small onion, minced
4 parsley sprigs, minced
1-1/2 cups fresh bread crumbs
1 egg
1 teaspoon Worcestershire sauce
1 teaspoon salt
Freshly ground pepper

This meat loaf is also delicious cold in sandwiches or with salad. Serve hot with ratatouille and steamed new potatoes.

1. Grease a 3-cup metal bowl or mold; set aside. In a large bowl, combine all ingredients.
2. Pack meat mixture into greased bowl or mold. Cover with buttered waxed paper and foil; seal well.
3. Place bowl or mold in a large saucepan. Add enough boiling water to saucepan to cover two-thirds of bowl or mold. Cover; steam over medium heat 2 hours. Remove bowl or mold from water. Cool 30 minutes. Refrigerate overnight, or freeze.
To freeze: If desired, turn out meat loaf; wrap in plastic wrap and foil. Or leave in bowl or mold; cover with fresh foil. Label. Freeze up to 3 weeks. Thaw about 6 hours in refrigerator.
To serve immediately or after refrigerating or thawing: Slice to serve cold. To serve warm, replace in bowl or mold. Cover; steam 1 hour. Makes 4 servings.

Left to right: Spaghetti Layer Bake, Meat Loaf

Ham Quiche

Basic pastry, page 27

Filling:
1-1/2 cups diced cooked ham
1 onion, chopped
1 large tomato, diced
2 tablespoons chopped fresh mixed herbs,
   any combination
1 cup shredded Swiss or Gruyère cheese (4 oz.)
3 eggs
1 cup half and half

1. Prepare Basic Pastry through step 3, page 27.
2. Preheat oven to 375F (190C).
3. In a medium bowl, combine ham, onion, tomato and herbs. Sprinkle half of cheese in bottom of cooled pastry shell. Spoon ham mixture over cheese. In a medium bowl, beat eggs; beat in half and half until blended. Pour egg mixture into pastry shell; sprinkle remaining cheese on top.
4. Bake in preheated oven 40 to 50 minutes or until center is set. Remove from oven; cool on a wire rack. Refrigerate overnight, or freeze.
To freeze: Open freeze cooled quiche in pan. Remove from pan, if desired. Wrap in foil; label. Freeze up to 2 months. Thaw unwrapped quiche at room temperature 2 to 3 hours.
To serve immediately or after refrigerating or thawing: Serve cold or heat in preheated 350F (175C) oven 15 to 20 minutes or until warm. Makes 4 to 6 servings.

Left to right: Ham Quiche, Chicken & Asparagus Turnovers

Chicken & Asparagus Turnovers

Pastry:
2-1/4 cups all-purpose flour
1 teaspoon baking powder
1 teaspoon salt
3/4 cup vegetable shortening
6 tablespoons iced water

Filling:
1 (8-oz.) can cut asparagus
Milk
1 tablespoon butter or margarine
1 tablespoon all-purpose flour
1-1/2 cups diced cooked chicken
Salt
Freshly ground pepper
1 egg yolk beaten with 1 tablespoon milk for glaze

---

1. To prepare pastry, in a medium bowl, combine flour, baking powder and salt. Cut in shortening with pastry blender or 2 knives until mixture resembles coarse crumbs.
2. Sprinkle crumb mixture with water; toss with a fork until mixture begins to stick together. Gather pastry into a ball. Divide pastry into 4 equal pieces.
3. To prepare filling, drain asparagus, reserving liquid. Add enough milk to liquid to measure 2/3 cup; set aside.
4. Melt butter or margarine in a small saucepan over low heat. Stir in flour; cook 1 minute. Gradually stir in milk mixture; cook until sauce is thickened, stirring constantly. Set aside to cool. Stir in drained asparagus, chicken, salt and pepper.
5. Roll out each pastry piece on a lightly floured surface to a 7-inch circle. Spoon 1/4 of filling onto center of each pastry circle. Brush pastry edges with water; fold pastry over filling to make half-moons. Flute pastry edges to seal. Prick tops lightly with a fork. Refrigerate overnight, or freeze.
To freeze: Place filled unbaked turnovers on an ungreased baking sheet; open freeze. When frozen, place in a plastic freezer bag. Seal and label. Freeze up to 1 month. Do not thaw before baking.
To serve immediately or after refrigerating or freezing: Preheat oven to 400F (205C). Unwrap frozen turnovers; place on an ungreased baking sheet. Brush tops with egg-yolk glaze. Bake frozen turnovers 40 to 45 minutes or until tops are golden brown. Bake refrigerated turnovers 20 to 25 minutes. Serve warm. Makes 4 servings.

Variation
Prepare pastry as directed above. Melt 2 tablespoons butter or margarine in a medium saucepan. Add 1 chopped onion; sauté until transparent. Add 1/2 pound lean ground beef; sauté until no longer pink. Drain off fat. Stir in 1 large diced, cooked potato. Season with 1 tablespoon chopped fresh dill or 1 teaspoon dried dill weed, salt and pepper. Fill turnovers and bake as above.

Spinach & Bacon Quiche

Basic Pastry:
1-1/2 cups sifted all-purpose flour
1/2 teaspoon salt
1/2 cup butter, margarine or vegetable shortening
1 egg, slightly beaten
2 to 3 tablespoons iced water

Filling:
2 tablespoons butter or margarine
1 medium onion, chopped
1 (10-oz.) pkg. frozen chopped spinach, thawed, drained
Salt
Freshly ground pepper
Freshly grated nutmeg
6 crisp-cooked bacon slices, crumbled
1 cup finely shredded Swiss or Gruyère cheese (4 oz.)
3 eggs
1 cup half and half

---

1. Preheat oven to 400F (205C).
2. To make pastry, in a medium bowl, combine flour and salt. With a pastry blender or 2 knives, cut in butter, margarine or shortening until mixture resembles coarse crumbs. In a small bowl, blend egg and 2 tablespoons water. Sprinkle egg mixture over flour mixture, tossing with a fork until mixture begins to stick together. Add remaining water, if necessary. Gather pastry into a ball.
3. Roll out pastry on a lightly floured surface to 1/8 inch thick. Line a 9-inch flan pan with a removable bottom with pastry. Prick pastry with fork. Line pastry with foil; fill with pie weights or dried beans. Bake in preheated oven 10 minutes. Remove foil and pie weights or beans; bake 5 minutes longer. Cool on a wire rack.
4. Reduce oven temperature to 375F (190C). Melt butter or margarine in a medium skillet over medium heat. Add onion; sauté until transparent. Stir in spinach. Season with salt, pepper and nutmeg. Set aside to cool.
5. Sprinkle bacon and 1/2 of cheese in bottom of cooled pastry shell. Spoon spinach mixture over cheese. In a small bowl, beat eggs with a whisk; beat in half and half until blended; pour into pastry. Top with remaining cheese.
6. Bake in preheated oven 40 to 50 minutes or until center is set. Cool baked quiche on a wire rack. Refrigerate overnight, or freeze.
To freeze: Open freeze cooled quiche. Remove quiche from pan, if desired. Wrap in foil; label. Freeze up to 2 months. Thaw unwrapped quiche at room temperature 3 to 4 hours.
To serve immediately or after refrigerating or thawing: Serve cold or heat in preheated 350F (175C) oven 15 to 20 minutes or until warm. Makes 4 to 6 servings.

Sausage & Rice

2 tablespoons butter or margarine
1 tablespoon vegetable oil
1 large onion, chopped
1 cup uncooked long-grain white rice
2-1/4 cups chicken stock
1/4 cup whole-kernel corn
1/4 cup raisins
8 oz. Polish sausage, sliced
Salt
Freshly ground pepper

To serve:
2 small sweet pickles, chopped
1 hard-cooked egg, chopped

---

1. Heat butter or margarine and oil in a medium saucepan over medium heat. Add onion; sauté 5 minutes or until softened.
2. Stir in rice and stock; bring to a boil. Cover; simmer about 25 minutes or until rice is tender and stock has been absorbed. Stir occasionally.
3. Add corn, raisins, sausage, salt and pepper. Cool 30 minutes. Refrigerate overnight, or freeze.
To freeze: Pack in a rigid freezer container. Cover and label. Freeze up to 2 months. Thaw at room temperature 3 to 4 hours.
To serve immediately or after refrigerating or thawing: Spoon into an baking dish; cover. Heat in a preheated 350F (175C) oven 1 hour or until heated through, stirring occasionally. Stir in pickles; sprinkle with chopped egg. Serve with a green salad. Makes 4 servings.

Savory Hamburger Mix

3 lb. lean ground beef
2 large onions, chopped
3 tablespoons bread crumbs
1/2 teaspoon Italian seasoning
2 teaspoons salt
Freshly ground pepper
1/2 cup beef stock

---

1. In a large skillet over medium heat, sauté beef, without added fat, 2 minutes. Add onions; sauté until beef is browned and onion is tender. Stir frequently to separate beef.
2. Add bread crumbs, Italian seasoning, salt and pepper. Cool 30 minutes. Refrigerate overnight, or freeze.
To freeze: Pack cooled meat mixture in 3 individual freezer containers. Cover and label. Freeze up to 2 months. Thaw overnight in refrigerator.
To serve immediately or after refrigerating or thawing: Use as a filling for Stuffed Peppers, page 16. Do not refreeze once mixture has thawed. Mixture can also be added to tomato sauce for a meat-and-tomato spaghetti sauce.

Spanish Rice

2/3 cup uncooked long-grain white rice
2 tablespoons vegetable oil
1 large onion, sliced
8 oz. tomatoes, peeled, quartered
1 cup chopped cooked roast beef
2 oz. mushrooms, chopped
2 tablespoons tomato paste
1/2 teaspoon dried leaf oregano
Salt
Freshly ground pepper
1/2 cup shredded Cheddar cheese (2 oz.)

---

1. Cook rice according to package directions until barely tender.
2. Heat oil in a large skillet over medium heat. Add onion; sauté until lightly browned. Stir in tomatoes, beef and mushrooms; cook 5 minutes.
3. Stir in tomato paste, oregano, cooked rice, salt and pepper. Cool 30 minutes. Refrigerate overnight, or freeze.
To freeze: Put into a rigid freezer container. Cover and label. Freeze up to 1 month. Thaw at room temperature about 3 hours.
To serve immediately or after refrigerating or thawing: Put into an ovenproof dish; sprinkle cheese on top. Bake in a preheated 375F (190C) oven about 40 minutes or until heated through. Serve with a green salad. Makes 4 servings.

Variation
Substitute any cooked meat or smoked sausage for roast beef.

Chicken Stir-Fry

1 red bell pepper, cut into strips
1 cauliflower, broken into cauliflowerets
2 celery stalks, cut into 1/4-inch slices
6 green onions, cut into 3/4-inch lengths
2 small zucchini, cut into 1/4-inch slices
2 tablespoons butter or margarine
1 tablespoon vegetable oil
4 boneless chicken breasts, skinned, cut into strips
4 oz. button mushrooms, halved

To serve:
2 tablespoons butter or margarine
1 tablespoon vegetable oil
2 teaspoons cornstarch
1 teaspoon sugar
2 teaspoons soy sauce
1/4 teaspoon dried leaf thyme
Salt
Freshly ground black pepper
Hot cooked rice or noodles

The secret of this dish is to keep the vegetables very crisp. This is a good opportunity to use up small amounts of raw vegetables; vary mixture accordingly. By blanching and freezing these vegetables, they will not be wasted.

1. Bring a saucepan of lightly salted water to a boil. Add bell pepper, cauliflowerets, celery, green onions and zucchini; bring to a boil. Drain immediately; cool blanched vegetables in iced water. Drain thoroughly. Spread drained vegetables on a baking sheet.
2. Heat butter or margarine and oil in a large skillet over medium heat. Add chicken; sauté 3 minutes. Add mushrooms; sauté 1 minute. With a slotted spoon, place sautéed chicken and mushrooms on baking sheet. Cool. Refrigerate overnight, or freeze. If refrigerating, do not spread chicken and vegetables on baking sheets; place in a covered container.
To freeze: Open freeze on baking sheets. When frozen, pack together in a rigid freezer container. Cover and label. Return to freezer up to 3 months. Cook without thawing.
To serve after refrigerating or freezing: Heat butter or margarine and oil in a skillet or wok over medium heat. Add frozen chicken and vegetables; stir-fry 5 minutes. If refrigerated, cook until hot. In a small bowl, combine cornstarch, sugar, soy sauce and thyme; add to skillet or wok. Cook until thickened, stirring constantly. Season with salt and pepper. Serve with hot cooked rice or noodles. Makes 4 servings.

Left to right: Spanish Rice, Chicken Stir-Fry

Main Dishes

Old-Fashioned Chicken Pie

Basic Pastry, page 27

6 tablespoons butter or margarine
1 onion, chopped
8 oz. mushrooms, thinly sliced
1/4 cup all-purpose flour
1-1/2 cups milk
1 cup chicken stock
2 cups diced cooked potatoes
2-1/2 cups diced cooked chicken
Salt
Freshly ground pepper
1 egg beaten with 1 tablespoon milk for glaze

---

1. Prepare Basic Pastry through step 2, page 27.
2. For filling, melt 2 tablespoons butter or margarine in a medium skillet over medium heat. Add onion; sauté until transparent. Add mushrooms; sauté 5 minutes. Set aside.
3. Melt remaining 1/4 cup butter or margarine in a large saucepan. Stir in flour; cook over low heat 1 minute, stirring constantly. Gradually stir in milk and stock or bouillon; cook over low heat until mixture is thickened, stirring constantly. Stir in reserved mushroom mixture, potatoes, chicken, salt and pepper. Spoon into a deep 9-inch pie plate or 2-quart casserole; set aside.
4. Preheat oven to 400F (205C). Roll out dough on a lightly floured surface to an 11-inch circle. Carefully fold dough over rolling pin; place over chicken filling. Trim excess dough; reserve for decoration. Crimp and flute pastry edge.
5. Gather dough scraps into a ball. Roll out dough to 1/8 inch thick. Cut out oval shapes as pictured for decoration. Make a hole in center of pie for a pie bird, or cut steam vent in center. Brush bottoms of decorations with water; place around center vent. Brush with egg mixture.
6. Place pie on a baking sheet. Bake in preheated oven 25 to 30 minutes or until pastry is golden brown. Cool on a wire rack. Refrigerate overnight, or freeze.
To freeze: Open freeze. When frozen, wrap in foil; label. Freeze up to 3 months. Thaw unwrapped pie in refrigerator overnight.
To serve after refrigerating or thawing: Place unwrapped pie on a baking sheet; heat in preheated 350F (175C) oven about 30 minutes or until hot and bubbly. If necessary, cover crust with foil to keep it from overbrowning. Makes 1 pie.

Golden Chicken Casserole

1 (15-oz.) can tomatoes
1/4 cup all-purpose flour
Salt
Freshly ground black pepper
1 (2-1/2- to 3-lb.) chicken, cut into quarters
1/4 cup vegetable oil
2 tablespoons butter or margarine
1 large onion, quartered, sliced
1 teaspoon turmeric
1 cup cider or apple juice
1/2 cup whole-kernel corn
1 small yellow bell pepper, sliced
1 small red bell pepper, sliced
1 Golden Delicious apple, cored, sliced

Turmeric has very little flavor, but gives a glowing golden color to this casserole. Yellow bell peppers are available in many large supermarkets. If they are not available, use a green bell pepper.

1. Preheat oven to 350F (175C). Drain tomatoes, reserving juice. Set tomatoes aside.
2. In a plastic bag, combine flour, salt and black pepper. Add chicken; shake to coat. Heat oil in a large skillet over medium heat. When oil is hot, add coated chicken; sauté until lightly browned on all sides. Using tongs, place browned chicken in a 2-quart casserole.
3. Add butter or margarine to skillet. Add onion; sauté until golden. Stir in any remaining seasoned flour and turmeric; cook 1 minute, stirring constantly.
4. Stir in reserved tomato juice and cider or apple juice. Cook until thickened, stirring constantly.
5. Cut drained tomatoes into quarters. Add tomato quarters, corn, bell peppers and apple to casserole. Pour sauce over chicken and vegetables. Cover casserole; bake in preheated oven about 40 minutes or until chicken is tender. Serve immediately, or cool 30 minutes. Refrigerate overnight, or freeze.
To freeze: Pack cooled chicken mixture into a rigid freezer container or freeze in casserole. Cover and label. Freeze up to 2 months. Thaw at room temperature 3 to 4 hours.
To serve after refrigerating or thawing: Return to casserole, if necessary. Cover and heat in a preheated 350F (175C) oven about 30 minutes. Taste and adjust seasoning. Makes 4 servings.

Top to bottom: Old-Fashioned Chicken Pie, Golden Chicken Casserole

Shepherd's Pie

1/3 recipe Savory Hamburger Mix, page 28
2 carrots, shredded
1/2 cup fresh or frozen green peas
2 celery stalks, sliced
2 tomatoes, sliced
4-1/2 cups diced, peeled potatoes,
   cooked (1-1/2 lb.)
2 tablespoons butter or margarine
2 tablespoons milk
Salt
Freshly ground pepper
Vegetable oil

1. In a large bowl, combine beef mixture, carrots, peas and celery. Spoon into a shallow 1-quart casserole. Cover with tomato slices.

2. In a large bowl, using a potato masher, mash potatoes with butter or margarine and milk until light and fluffy. Season with salt and pepper; spread mashed potatoes over tomatoes. Using the tines of a fork, decorate potatoes. Cool 30 minutes. Refrigerate overnight, or freeze.

To freeze: Cover cooled casserole with foil; label. Freeze up to 3 months. Thaw at room temperature 3 to 4 hours.

To serve immediately or after refrigerating or thawing: Uncover; brush potatoes with a little oil. Bake in a preheated 375F (190C) oven about 1-1/4 hours or until heated through and potatoes are browned.

Variation

Substitute 1 (8-ounce) can baked beans in tomato sauce, for carrots, peas and celery. Stir 1/2 cup (2 ounces) shredded Cheddar cheese into mashed potatoes.

Left to right: Shepherd's Pie, Turkey & Noodle Ring

Turkey & Noodle Ring

8 oz. egg noodles
Salt
5 tablespoons butter or margarine

Filling:
1 cup chicken stock
1 bay leaf
1 onion
4 whole cloves
3 tablespoons butter or margarine
1/3 cup all-purpose flour
3/4 cup milk
Salt
Freshly ground pepper
1-1/2 cups cubed cooked turkey
2 canned pimentos, drained, sliced
1 tablespoon chopped fresh parsley
3 tablespoons half and half

To garnish:
Finely chopped fresh parsley

1. Cook noodles in a large saucepan according to package directions until almost tender. Drain well; return to saucepan. Add salt and butter or margarine; stir until melted. Pack buttered noodles into a ring mold; set aside to cool.
2. In a medium saucepan, combine stock, bay leaf and onion studded with cloves. Bring to a boil; reduce heat. Simmer 10 minutes. Strain stock, discarding onion and bay leaf.
3. To make filling, in a medium saucepan, melt butter or margarine. Stir in flour; cook 1 minute, stirring constantly. Whisk in seasoned stock and milk. Cook until thickened and smooth, stirring constantly. Stir in salt, pepper, turkey, pimentos and parsley. Simmer 5 minutes; cool 30 minutes. Refrigerate overnight, or freeze.
To freeze: Pack cooled filling into a rigid freezer container. Cover and label. Wrap ring mold in foil; label. Freeze filling and noodles up to 2 months. Thaw ring mold at room temperature 3 to 4 hours. Thaw filling only until it can be removed from container.
To serve immediately or after refrigerating or thawing: Unwrap ring mold; place in a roasting pan. Add enough boiling water to pan to come half-way up side of mold. Bake in a preheated 325F (165C) oven about 30 minutes or until heated through. Meanwhile, place filling in a saucepan; bring to a boil over medium heat, stirring occasionally. Stir in half and half; heat but do not boil. Turn out noodle ring onto a heated serving dish. Spoon hot filling into center. Sprinkle with chopped parsley. Makes 4 servings.

Filled Pasta Shells

1 lb. lean ground beef
2 tablespoons butter or margarine
1 onion, chopped
2 eggs, beaten
2 cups shredded mozzarella cheese (8 oz).
8 oz. cup ricotta cheese (1 cup)
3/4 cup grated Parmesan cheese (2-1/4 oz.)
1/4 cup dry bread crumbs
1 teaspoon Italian seasoning
Salt
Freshly ground pepper
6 cups spaghetti sauce, homemade or prepared
1 (12-oz.) pkg. jumbo pasta shells, cooked, drained

1. In a medium skillet, sauté beef, without added fat, until no longer pink. Drain off fat; spoon cooked beef into a large bowl. Melt butter or margarine in same skillet. Add onion; cook until transparent. Stir cooked onion, eggs, mozzarella cheese, ricotta cheese, 1/2 cup Parmesan cheese, bread crumbs, Italian seasoning, salt and pepper into cooked beef.
2. Preheat oven to 350F (175C). Spoon about 1 cup spaghetti sauce over bottom of an 11" x 7" baking dish. Repeat with a second baking dish.
3. Fill cooked shells with meat filling; place 15 filled shells in a single layer in each dish. Pour 2 cups sauce over filled shells in each dish. Sprinkle each dish with 2 tablespoons of remaining Parmesan cheese.
4. Bake in preheated oven 25 to 30 minutes or until cheese is melted. Serve immediately or cool. Refrigerate overnight, or freeze.
To freeze: Wrap in foil; label. Freeze up to 3 months. Thaw overnight in refrigerator.
To serve after refrigerating or thawing: Heat in a preheated 350F (175C) oven 30 minutes or until sauce is bubbling and shells are heated through. Makes 2 casseroles, 6 servings each.

Winter Beef Stew

3 tablespoons vegetable oil
1-1/2 lb. beef stew cubes
2 onions, cut into 8 pieces each
2 carrots, sliced
1 parsnip, chopped
1 turnip, chopped
1 celery stalk, sliced
2 tablespoons all-purpose flour
1 (8-oz.) can tomatoes
1/2 teaspoon Italian seasoning
1 teaspoon prepared brown mustard
2 cups beef stock
Salt
Freshly ground pepper

To serve:
2 tablespoons sherry
Chopped fresh parsley

---

1. Heat oil in a large heavy saucepan. Add beef cubes in 3 batches; sauté until browned. Using a slotted spoon, remove browned cubes from pan. Drain on paper towels.
2. Add vegetables to pan; sauté gently 5 minutes.
3. Stir in flour; stirring often, cook 5 minutes or until flour is golden brown.
4. Stir in undrained tomatoes, Italian seasoning, mustard and stock. Bring to a boil; cook until thickened and smooth. Season with salt and pepper.
5. Return beef to pan. Cover; simmer about 1-1/2 hours or until beef is tender, stirring occasionally. Cool 30 minutes. Refrigerate overnight, or freeze.
To freeze: Pack cooled stew into a rigid freezer container. Cover and label. Freeze up to 2 months. Thaw at room temperature 4 to 6 hours.
To serve after refrigerating or thawing: Lift off and discard any fat. Bring stew to a boil in a large saucepan, stirring occasionally. Add sherry; adjust seasoning. Sprinkle with parsley. Makes 4 to 6 servings.

Variation

Beef & Mushroom Crumble: Substitute 8 ounces chopped mushrooms for carrots, parsnip, turnip and celery. Use only 1/2 cup stock. After cooking, cool stew. Spoon into a casserole. Top with *Crumble Topping.* To make Crumble Topping, in a medium bowl, cut 5 tablespoons firm butter or margarine into 1-1/4 cups all-purpose flour; season with salt and pepper. Stir in 1/2 cup (2 ounces) shredded Cheddar cheese. Sprinkle topping over stew.
To freeze: Cover and label. Freeze up to 2 months. Thaw at room temperature 4 to 5 hours.
To serve after thawing: Uncover; bake thawed casserole in a preheated 375F (190C) oven 50 minutes or until topping is golden brown.

Chili con Carne

2 lb. lean ground beef
2 large onions, finely chopped
2 garlic cloves, crushed
6 tablespoons all-purpose flour
2 tablespoons tomato paste
2 (16-oz.) cans tomatoes with juice, chopped
2 (15-oz.) cans kidney beans, undrained
2 teaspoons dried leaf oregano
1 teaspoon ground cumin
2 tablespoons chili powder
Hot-pepper sauce

---

1. In a large heavy saucepan over medium heat, sauté beef, without added fat, until no longer pink. Add onions and garlic; sauté until onion is tender. Drain off fat.
2. Stir flour into cooked beef mixture. Cook 1 minute, stirring constantly. Stir in tomato paste, tomatoes with juice, kidney beans, oregano, cumin, chili powder and hot-pepper sauce to taste.
3. Simmer 30 minutes. Cool 30 minutes. Refrigerate overnight, or freeze.
To freeze: Pack cooled chili into 2 rigid freezer containers. Cover and label. Freeze up to 1 month. Thaw overnight in refrigerator.
To serve after refrigerating or thawing: In a large saucepan over medium heat, bring chili to a boil, stirring frequently. Makes 8 servings.

Spiced Brisket

1 (2-lb.) rolled beef brisket
2-1/2 cups beef stock
1 small onion, sliced
6 strips lemon peel
1 bay leaf
1 tablespoon pickling spice
Salt
Freshly ground pepper
3 fresh parsley sprigs

---

1. Preheat oven to 325F (165C).
2. Place roast into a deep casserole or Dutch oven. Add stock, onion, lemon peel and bay leaf. Tie pickling spice in cheesecloth; add to roast. Add salt, pepper and parsley sprigs.
3. Cover; roast in preheated oven about 2 hours or until roast is tender.
4. Carefully lift out roast; place in a bowl or dish that will hold it snugly. Cover with a plate; place a heavy weight on plate. Refrigerate overnight.
5. Strain cooking liquid, discarding vegetables; reserve for another use, if desired.
To serve after refrigerating: Thinly slice roast. Serve with pickles or salads. Roast is excellent for sandwiches. Makes 6 to 8 servings.

Beef Burgundy

2 tablespoons vegetable oil
1-1/2 lb. beef-round steak, cut in 1-inch cubes
2 medium onions, chopped
2 garlic cloves, crushed
1 cup red wine
3/4 cup beef stock
1 bay leaf
1 teaspoon Italian seasoning
Salt
Freshly ground pepper
6 oz. mushrooms, sliced
3 tablespoons all-purpose flour

This is an excellent dish to have on hand for unexpected guests. Double recipe, if desired.

1. Heat oil in a large heavy saucepan. Add beef; sauté until browned. Add onions and garlic; sauté until softened.
2. Add wine, 1/2 cup stock, bay leaf and Italian seasoning. Season with salt and pepper. Cover; simmer over low heat 40 minutes. Add mushrooms; simmer 15 minutes longer or until beef is tender.
3. In a small bowl, blend flour and remaining stock into a paste. Stir into hot stew. Cook until thickened, stirring frequently. Discard bay leaf. Cool 30 minutes. Refrigerate overnight, or freeze.
To freeze: Spoon stew into a rigid freezer container. Cover and label. Freeze up to 2 months. Thaw overnight in refrigerator.
To serve after refrigerating or thawing: Heat in a large saucepan until hot and bubbling. Serve with French bread and a green salad. Makes 4 servings.

Clockwise from upper left: Chili con Carne; Confetti Rice without corn, page 36; Beef Burgundy

Sweet & Sour Ham Steaks

4 (4- to 6-oz.) ham steaks
Vegetable oil
4 teaspoons brown sugar

Sauce:
1 (8-oz.) can pineapple chunks (juice pack)
1 tablespoon vegetable oil
1 onion, finely chopped
1 tablespoon all-purpose flour
1 tablespoon soy sauce
1 tablespoon wine vinegar
1 tablespoon ketchup
Freshly ground pepper

Confetti Rice:
1 cup uncooked long-grain white rice
1/4 cup frozen or fresh peas
1/4 cup frozen or canned whole-kernel corn, if desired
2 tablespoons water

---

1. Preheat broiler. Place ham steaks on a rack in a broiler pan. Brush lightly with oil; broil under preheated broiler 5 minutes.
2. Turn steaks. Brush with oil; sprinkle with brown sugar. Broil until sugar melts and caramelizes.
3. To make sauce, drain juice from pineapple into a measuring cup. Add enough water to make 1 cup.
4. Heat oil in a medium saucepan. Add onion; sauté until softened. Stir in flour; cook 1 minute, stirring constantly.
5. Stir juice mixture, soy sauce, vinegar and ketchup into flour mixture. Cook, stirring constantly, until sauce thickens. Stir in pineapple chunks. Season with pepper. Pour sauce over broiled ham; cool. Refrigerate overnight, or freeze.
6. To make Confetti Rice, cook rice according to package directions until almost tender. Stir in peas and corn, if desired. Cook until rice is tender and liquid is absorbed. Cool. Refrigerate overnight, or freeze.
To freeze: Pack ham and sauce into a rigid freezer container. Cover and label. Pack cooled rice into a rigid freezer container. Cover and label. Freeze ham and rice up to 1 month. Thaw 2 to 3 hours at room temperature.
To serve after refrigerating or thawing: Place ham and sauce into an ovenproof dish. Cover; heat in a preheated 350F (175C) oven until hot and bubbling. Heat rice mixture in a medium saucepan with 2 tablespoons water. Cook over low heat until water is absorbed and rice is hot. Serve with ham. Makes 4 servings.

Clockwise from left: Sweet & Sour Ham Steaks with Confetti Rice, Pork Paprika, Pork Patties & Red Cabbage

Pork Paprika

2 tablespoons vegetable oil
1/4 cup butter or margarine
1 (1-lb.) pork-loin tenderloin, sliced
1 onion, chopped
1 garlic clove, crushed
2 tablespoons paprika
3 tablespoons all-purpose flour
1/2 cup cider or white wine
1/2 cup beef stock
1 tablespoon tomato paste
Salt
Freshly ground pepper
6 oz. small button mushrooms, halved

To serve:
1/2 cup dairy sour cream

Pork Patties & Red Cabbage

1 lb. lean ground pork
1 medium onion, finely chopped
2 tablespoons dry bread crumbs
1 teaspoon dried leaf thyme
1 tablespoon finely chopped fresh parsley
1 egg, beaten
Salt
Freshly ground pepper
1/4 cup butter or margarine
2 tablespoons vegetable oil

Red Cabbage:
3 tablespoons butter or margarine
2 lb. red cabbage, finely sliced
1/4 cup packed brown sugar
1/4 cup water
1/4 cup wine vinegar
Salt
Freshly ground pepper
1 cooking apple, peeled, cored, chopped

---

1. In a large bowl, combine pork, onion, bread crumbs, thyme, parsley, egg, salt and pepper until blended. With floured hands, shape pork mixture into 8 oval patties. Chill 1 hour.
2. Heat butter or margarine and oil in a large skillet. Add patties, 4 at a time; sauté over a medium heat about 8 minutes per side or until well browned. Remove browned patties from pan; sauté remaining patties. Cool. Refrigerate overnight, or freeze.
3. To make red cabbage, melt butter or margarine in a heavy saucepan. Add cabbage, brown sugar, water, vinegar, salt and pepper. Cover tightly; cook over low heat about 30 minutes, shaking pan and stirring occasionally.
4. Add apple; cook 15 minutes longer. Cool. Refrigerate overnight, or freeze.
To freeze: Pack pork patties and cabbage into separate freezer containers. Cover and label. Freeze up to 1 month. Thaw at room temperature 2 to 3 hours.
To serve after refrigerating or thawing: Place cabbage in a casserole. Cover; heat in a preheated 350F (175C) oven about 30 minutes or until hot. Place pork patties on a greased baking sheet. Heat in same oven 30 minutes. Serve with boiled new potatoes tossed in melted butter and finely chopped parsley. Makes 4 servings.

Variation
Substitute *Mock Sauerkraut* for *Red Cabbage.* To make Mock Sauerkraut, finely shred white cabbage. Cook as above except substitute 1 tablespoon granulated sugar for 1/4 cup brown sugar; add 1/2 teaspoon caraway seeds. Be careful that cabbage does not brown.

---

1. Heat oil and butter or margarine in a large heavy saucepan. Add pork slices; brown on both sides. Using tongs, remove from pan.
2. Add onion, garlic and paprika to pan; sauté about 2 minutes. Stir in flour; cook 1 minute, stirring constantly.
3. Stir in cider or wine, stock and tomato paste. Bring to a boil; cook until thickened and smooth, stirring constantly.
4. Season with salt and pepper. Return pork to saucepan; cover. Simmer 15 minutes. Add mushrooms; cook 5 minutes. Cool 30 minutes. Refrigerate overnight, or freeze.
To freeze: Pack cooled pork and sauce into a rigid freezer container. Cover and label. Freeze up to 1 month. Thaw at room temperature 3 to 4 hours.
To serve immediately or after refrigerating or thawing: Bring pork and sauce to a boil in a large saucepan, stirring occasionally. Stir in sour cream; heat but do not boil. Adjust seasonings. Serve with small boiled potatoes and green vegetables. Makes 4 servings.

Pork & Pineapple Casserole

2 tablespoons vegetable oil
1-1/2 lb. lean pork cubes, trimmed
1 tablespoon cornstarch
1 tablespoon sugar
1/4 cup water
1/4 cup soy sauce
1/4 cup red-wine vinegar
2 tablespoons dry sherry
1 tablespoon Worcestershire sauce
1/2 teaspoon ground ginger
1 (15-1/4-oz.) can pineapple chunks (juice pack)
1 red or green bell pepper, cut into 1-inch pieces
1 cup macadamia nuts

1. Preheat oven to 350F (175C).
2. Heat oil in a medium skillet. Add pork; sauté over medium heat until browned on all sides. Using a slotted spoon, place browned pork in a 1-1/2-quart casserole.
3. In a medium bowl, combine cornstarch and sugar. Stir in water until smooth. Stir in soy sauce, vinegar, sherry, Worcestershire sauce and ginger. Drain syrup from pineapple; stir syrup into cornstarch mixture. Set pineapple aside.
4. Pour cornstarch mixture over browned pork; stir until pork is coated. Cover; bake in preheated oven 30 minutes.
5. Add reserved pineapple, bell pepper and macadamia nuts to pork. Stir well; replace cover. Bake 30 minutes longer or until pork is thoroughly cooked. Cool 30 minutes. Refrigerate overnight, or freeze.
To freeze: Wrap cooled casserole in foil; label. Freeze up to 1 month. Thaw at room temperature 3 to 4 hours.
To serve after refrigerating or thawing: Cover; bake in a preheated 350F (175C) oven 20 minutes or until heated through. Makes 4 to 6 servings.

Left to right: Leek Pie, Lamb with Pineapple

Leek Pie

Pastry:
1-1/2 cups all-purpose flour
1/4 teaspoon salt
1/2 cup butter or margarine
4 to 5 tablespoons iced water

Filling:
6 tablespoons butter or margarine
6 to 8 medium leeks, rinsed, trimmed, sliced
3 tablespoons all-purpose flour
3/4 cup chicken stock
3/4 cup milk
2 eggs
6 crisp-cooked bacon slices, crumbled
Salt
Freshly ground pepper
Milk

---

1. To make pastry, in a medium bowl, combine flour and salt. With a pastry blender or 2 knives, cut in butter or margarine until mixture resembles coarse crumbs. Sprinkle with water, 1 tablespoon at a time, tossing with a fork until mixture holds together. Form dough into a ball. Wrap in waxed paper or plastic wrap; refrigerate 30 minutes.
2. To make filling, melt 3 tablespoons butter or margarine in a large skillet. Add leeks; sauté 5 minutes or until softened. Remove from heat; set aside.
3. Melt remaining 3 tablespoons butter or margarine in a medium saucepan. Stir in flour; cook 1 minute. Gradually stir in stock and 3/4 cup milk; bring to a boil, stirring constantly. In a small bowl, beat eggs with a whisk. Whisk 3 tablespoons sauce into beaten eggs until blended. Pour mixture back into saucepan; cook over low heat until sauce is thickened, stirring constantly. Do not boil. Remove from heat; stir in bacon and sautéed leeks. Season with salt and pepper. Cool. Spoon leek mixture into a 9-inch pie pan or 1-1/2-quart casserole.
4. Preheat oven to 400F (205C). Roll out dough on a lightly floured surface to an 11-inch circle. Fold dough over rolling pin; place over leek filling. Trim excess dough; reserve for decoration. Crimp and flute pastry edge.
5. Gather dough scraps into a ball; roll out to 1/8 inch thick. Cut out decorations. Make a hole in center of pie to let steam escape. Brush bottom of decorations with water; place on top of pie. Brush top of pie with milk.
6. Place pie on a baking sheet; bake in preheated oven 25 to 30 minutes or until pastry is golden brown. Cool completely on a wire rack. Refrigerate overnight, or freeze.
To freeze: Open freeze. When frozen, wrap in foil; label. Freeze up to 1 month. Thaw unwrapped pie at room temperature 3 to 4 hours.
To serve after refrigerating or thawing: Place on a baking sheet. Bake in a preheated 350F (175C) oven about 30 minutes or until hot and bubbly. Makes 6 servings.

Lamb with Pineapple

2 to 2-1/2 lb. lean lamb stew cubes
1 (8-oz.) can pineapple chunks (juice pack)
About 1 cup beef stock
2 tablespoons vegetable oil
12 small white onions
1/4 cup all-purpose flour
1/4 teaspoon Chinese five-spice powder
2 tablespoons tomato paste
Salt
Freshly ground pepper
8 oz. button mushrooms

To garnish:
Chopped fresh parsley

If five-spice powder is unavailable, substitute a pinch each of ground nutmeg and coriander, 1 to 2 teaspoons soy sauce and 1 tablespoon sherry.

1. Preheat oven to 350F (175C). If necessary, trim lamb. Drain juice from pineapple into a 2-cup measuring cup. Add enough stock to make 1-1/2 cups.
2. Heat oil in a large skillet. Add onions; sauté until lightly browned. Add lamb cubes; sauté until lightly browned. Using a slotted spoon, place browned onions and lamb in a 2-1/2-quart casserole.
3. Stir flour and five-spice powder into skillet; cook 1 minute, stirring constantly. Stir juice mixture into flour mixture. Cook until thickened and smooth, stirring constantly. Stir in tomato paste. Season with salt and pepper. Pour sauce over lamb and onions.
4. Cover; bake in preheated oven 1-1/4 hours or until lamb is tender. Stir in mushrooms and drained pineapple. Cool 30 minutes. Refrigerate overnight, or freeze.
To freeze: Pack cooled lamb mixture into a rigid freezer container. Cover and label. Freeze up to 1 month. Thaw overnight in refrigerator.
To serve after refrigerating or thawing: Return to casserole; cover. Bake in a preheated 350F (175C) oven about 45 minutes or until hot and bubbling. Adjust seasoning. Sprinkle with parsley. Serve with hot cooked rice and green vegetables. Makes 6 servings.

Variation
Substitute 1 (15-ounce) can lima beans with liquid, and 1 tablespoon chopped fresh mint for pineapple. Serve with chow-mein noodles.

Sausage-Stuffed Beef Rolls

4 oz. bulk pork sausage
1 egg, beaten
4 bread slices, made into bread crumbs
1 teaspoon Italian seasoning
1 teaspoon prepared brown mustard
Salt
Freshly ground pepper
1 (1-1/2-lb.) beef-flank steak
1 large potato, peeled, diced
2 carrots, sliced
1 parsnip, diced
1 turnip, diced
1 onion, chopped
2 tablespoons all-purpose flour
1 cup beef stock

---

1. Preheat oven to 325F (165C).
2. In a medium bowl, combine sausage, egg, bread crumbs, Italian seasoning, mustard, salt and pepper. Spread evenly over steak. Roll up steak from long side; tie with kitchen string.
3. Place all vegetables into a large roasting pan; sprinkle with flour, salt and pepper. Pour in stock. Lay stuffed steak on top.
4. Cover with foil; bake in preheated oven 2 hours. Cool 30 minutes. Refrigerate overnight, or freeze.
To freeze: Wrap cooled steak roll in foil; label. Pack vegetables into a rigid freezer container. Cover and label. Freeze up to 1 month. Thaw in refrigerator overnight.
To serve after refrigerating or thawing: Cut steak into thick slices. Place vegetables in an oval ovenproof serving dish; arrange steak slices on top. Cover with foil; heat in a preheated 350F (175C) oven about 30 minutes or until heated through. Makes 4 servings.

Beef Curry

1/4 cup vegetable oil
1 large onion, chopped
1 garlic clove, crushed
1 (1/2-inch) piece gingerroot, peeled, finely chopped
1/4 cup cream of coconut
2 to 4 teaspoons curry powder
2 cups beef stock
Salt
Freshly ground pepper
1 lb. beef stew cubes
1/4 teaspoon ground coriander
2 tablespoons apricot jam

Everyone who likes curry has their own favorite recipe. This basic sauce can be used with meat, shrimp or eggs. Add curry powder to taste.

1. Heat 2 tablespoons oil in a large saucepan. Add onion and garlic; sauté until lightly browned. Stir in ginger and cream of coconut; cook 2 minutes.
2. Stir in curry powder and stock. Season with salt and pepper. Bring to a boil; simmer 15 minutes.
3. Meanwhile, heat remaining oil in a large skillet. Add beef; season with salt, pepper and coriander. Sauté until well browned.
4. Place browned beef in sauce. Cook over low heat 1 hour or until beef is tender. Stir in jam. Cool 30 minutes. Refrigerate overnight, or freeze.
To freeze: Pack beef mixture into a rigid freezer container. Cover and label. Freeze up to 1 month. Thaw at room temperature 3 to 4 hours.
To serve after refrigerating or thawing: Heat beef curry in a saucepan. Bring to a boil, stirring occasionally. Adjust seasoning. Serve with hot cooked rice, sliced-tomato-and-onion salad and grated cucumber combined with plain yogurt. Makes 4 servings.

To make your own curry powder, combine 4 teaspoons ground coriander, 1 teaspoon ground turmeric, 2 teaspoons ground cumin, 1 teaspoon freshly ground pepper, 2 to 4 teaspoons chili powder and 1 teaspoon ground cloves. Or, if you have a spice mill, grind whole spices and combine as desired. Store curry powder in a tightly covered container.

Fresh gingerroot is much milder in flavor than ground ginger. To keep gingerroot fresh, store peeled slices covered with sherry in a tightly sealed jar 1 to 2 months. Or, open freeze grated or sliced fresh gingerroot on a baking sheet. When frozen, pack in a small plastic freezer bag. Freeze up to 3 months.

Pork & Potato Bake

2 carrots, chopped
1 small rutabaga, chopped
1 small parsnip, chopped
1 small turnip, chopped
1/2 teaspoon salt
Water
2 tablespoons vegetable oil
4 thick pork chops, trimmed
1 onion, chopped
Freshly ground pepper
4-1/2 cups sliced, peeled potatoes, cooked 5 minutes

1. Place carrots, rutabaga, parsnip, turnip and salt into a medium saucepan. Cover with water; bring to a boil. Simmer 3 minutes. Drain, reserving 1 cup liquid.
2. Place cooked vegetables in bottom of a 2-quart casserole.
3. Heat oil in a large skillet. Add chops; sauté 5 minutes on each side. Using tongs, remove browned chops from skillet; set aside. Add onion to skillet; sauté until softened.
4. Scatter cooked onion over vegetables in casserole. Lay browned chops on vegetables. Sprinkle with salt and pepper. Pour reserved cooking liquid over chops.
5. Cover chops with overlapping potato slices. Brush with drippings from skillet. Cool 30 minutes. Refrigerate overnight, or freeze.
To freeze: Cover casserole tightly. Label. Freeze up to 1 month. Thaw at room temperature 3 to 4 hours.
To serve after refrigerating or thawing: Uncover; bake in a preheated 325F (165C) oven 1 to 1-1/2 hours or until pork is tender and potatoes are tender and browned. Serve with a green vegetable. Makes 4 servings.

Sausage-Stuffed Beef Rolls

Chicken-Liver Pan-Fry

2 tablespoons vegetable oil
2 bacon slices, chopped
1 onion, finely chopped
1 small green bell pepper, sliced
1 lb. chicken livers, trimmed
4 oz. mushrooms, quartered
1 to 2 teaspoons rubbed sage

To serve:
6 tablespoons dry vermouth or white wine
Salt
Freshly ground pepper

---

1. Heat oil in a large skillet. Add bacon and onion; sauté until bacon is lightly browned.
2. Add bell pepper and chicken livers; sauté 5 minutes. Stir in mushrooms and sage; sauté 5 minutes longer. Cool 30 minutes. Refrigerate overnight, or freeze.
To freeze: Pack liver mixture in a rigid freezer container. Cover and label. Freeze up to 1 month. Thaw in refrigerator overnight.
To serve immediately or after refrigerating or thawing: Return to pan, add vermouth or wine. Bring to a boil, stirring occasionally. Season with salt and pepper. Serve with hot cooked white or brown rice and a green salad. Makes 4 servings.

Liver Stroganoff

1/4 cup butter or margarine
1 tablespoon vegetable oil
1 large onion, thinly sliced
1 lb. calves' liver, cut into thin strips
1 tablespoon tomato paste
1/2 cup beef stock
1 teaspoon prepared brown mustard

To serve:
1/2 cup dairy sour cream
Salt
Freshly ground pepper

---

1. Heat butter or margarine and oil in a large skillet. Add onion; sauté until softened.
2. Add liver; sauté about 5 minutes or until liver is barely done.
3. Stir in tomato paste and stock; cook 2 minutes. Stir in mustard. Cool 30 minutes. Refrigerate overnight, or freeze.
To freeze: Pack liver mixture in a rigid freezer container. Cover and label. Freeze up to 1 month. Thaw overnight in refrigerator.
To serve immediately or after refrigerating or thawing: Heat liver stroganoff in a medium saucepan. Bring to a boil, stirring frequently. Stir in sour cream; heat but do not boil. Season to taste with salt and pepper. Serve immediately with hot cooked noodles or rice. Makes 4 servings.

Left to right: Chicken-Liver Pan-Fry, Liver Stroganoff

Oxtail Stew with Dumplings

5 tablespoons all-purpose flour
Salt
Freshly ground pepper
1 oxtail, cut up
2 tablespoons vegetable oil
3 cups beef stock
1 tablespoon prepared horseradish
1 large onion, sliced
2 carrots, sliced
2 celery stalks, sliced
1 small parsnip, diced
1 bay leaf

Dumplings:
1 cup cake flour
2 teaspoons baking powder
1/2 teaspoon salt
1 teaspoon Italian seasoning
1 egg
Milk

Oxtail is an inexpensive cut that is ideally suited to braising. The meat becomes tender and the flavor is superb.

1. Preheat oven to 325F (165C).
2. In a plastic bag, combine flour, salt and pepper. Add oxtail pieces; shake to coat.

3. Heat oil in a large skillet. Add oxtail pieces; sauté until browned all over. With a slotted spoon, remove browned oxtail pieces; set aside.
4. Add any remaining seasoned flour to skillet; stirring, cook 1 minute or until browned. Stir in stock; stirring constantly, cook until thickened and smooth. Stir in horseradish.
5. Place all vegetables in bottom of a 2-quart casserole. Add bay leaf. Arrange browned oxtail pieces over vegetables.
6. Pour horseradish sauce over oxtail pieces. Cover; bake in preheated oven 3 hours. Cool; spoon off any fat from surface. Discard bay leaf.
7. To make dumplings, combine cake flour, baking powder, salt and Italian seasoning. Beat egg in a 1-cup measuring cup; add enough milk to make 1/2 cup. Stir egg mixture into dry ingredients. Add more milk, if necessary, but keep batter stiff. If refrigerating stew overnight before serving, make dumplings while stew heats.
To freeze: Put cooled stew into a rigid freezer container. Cover and label. Freeze up to 1 month. Drop dumplings by tablespoonfuls onto a greased baking sheet. Open freeze dumplings. When frozen, pack in a plastic bag or container; label. Freeze up to 1 month. Thaw stew overnight in refrigerator. Cook dumplings frozen.
To serve immediately or after refrigerating or thawing: Lift off and discard any fat. Return stew to casserole. Cover; bake in a preheated 350F (175C) oven about 1 hour or until hot and bubbly. Top with fresh or frozen dumplings; replace cover. Bake 20 minutes longer or until dumplings are firm when touched. Makes 4 servings.

Haddock & Anchovy Puff

1 (12-oz.) haddock fillet
1/2 cup milk
1/2 cup water
2 tablespoons butter
3 tablespoons all-purpose flour
4 anchovy fillets, chopped
1 hard-cooked egg, minced
Salt
Freshly ground pepper
1/2 (17-1/4-oz.) package frozen puff pastry, thawed
1 egg yolk beaten with 1 tablespoon water for glaze

If you find the salty flavor of anchovies too strong, use chopped parsley and some lemon peel instead. Mince the egg white, or it will be rubbery after freezing.

1. Place fish, milk and water in a medium saucepan. Cover; simmer 10 minutes.
2. Remove poached fish from pan; reserve cooking liquid in pan. Remove and discard skin and bones from fish. Flake fish.
3. Combine butter and flour into a paste. Cut in small pieces; stir into reserved cooking liquid. Bring to a boil, stirring until thickened and smooth. Stir in flaked fish, anchovies and hard-cooked egg. Season with salt and pepper.
4. Roll out pastry dough on a lightly floured board to a 12-inch square. Trim edges. Turn pastry so a corner is pointing toward you.
5. Put fish mixture in center of square. Fold pastry like an envelope. Fold the bottom corner to center, 2 side corners to center, then top corner down to cover. Brush all edges with beaten egg as you fold; press to seal. Refrigerate overnight, or freeze.
To freeze: Put pastry on a baking sheet; open freeze. When frozen, wrap in foil; label. Freeze up to 1 month. Thaw unwrapped filled pastry on a baking sheet at room temperature 2 to 3 hours.
To serve immediately or after refrigerating or thawing: Brush with egg-yolk glaze; bake in a preheated 400F (205C) oven 45 to 50 minutes or until raised, golden brown and heated through.

Top to bottom: Haddock & Anchovy Puff, Stuffed Fish Fillets

Stuffed Fish Fillets

4 (4- to 6-oz.) fish fillets with skin
Stuffing:
2 tablespoons butter or margarine
1 small onion, chopped
1 small cooking apple, peeled, cored, grated
Grated peel and juice of 1/2 lemon
1 tablespoon chopped parsley
1/4 cup dry bread crumbs
Salt
Freshly ground pepper
6 tablespoons apple juice

To garnish:
Lemon slices
Parsley sprigs

1. Preheat oven to 350F (175C). Wipe fillets with damp paper towels.
2. To make stuffing, melt butter or margarine in a medium skillet. Add onion; sauté until softened. Stir in apple, lemon peel, lemon juice, parsley, bread crumbs, salt and pepper.
3. Lay fillets on a flat surface, skin-side down. Divide stuffing among fillets; roll up, starting at tail end.
4. Put rolls into a freezer-to-oven dish large enough to hold rolls in 1 layer. Spoon apple juice over top.
5. Cover with buttered waxed paper and foil; bake in preheated oven about 15 minutes. Cool 30 minutes. Remove waxed paper and foil. Cover with fresh waxed paper and foil. Refrigerate overnight, or freeze.
To freeze: Label. Freeze up to 1 month. Do not thaw before reheating.
To serve after refrigerating or freezing: Heat frozen fish in a preheated 350F (175C) oven about 30 minutes or until heated through. If refrigerated, heat 10 to 15 minutes. Garnish with lemon slices and parsley. Makes 4 servings.

Smoky Fish Cakes

12 oz. smoked haddock or other smoked fish fillets
1/2 cup milk
2 tablespoons butter or margarine
3/4 cup mashed potatoes
1 tablespoon chopped parsley
Freshly ground pepper
1 small package onion-and-sour-cream-flavored potato chips
1/4 cup dry bread crumbs
1 egg, beaten
Vegetable oil for deep-frying

1. Place fish and milk in a medium saucepan. Simmer 10 minutes. Drain, reserving 2 tablespoons liquid. Remove and discard any skin and bones from poached fish; flake fish.
2. In a small bowl, beat reserved poaching liquid and butter or margarine into potatoes. Stir in flaked fish, parsley and pepper. With lightly floured hands, shape fish mixture into 8 round cakes. Refrigerate until firm.
3. Put potato chips into a plastic bag; finely crush with a rolling pin. In a shallow bowl, combine crushed chips and bread crumbs.
4. Dip fish cakes into beaten egg to coat; then press into crumb mixture. Refrigerate overnight, or freeze.
To freeze: Open freeze on a baking sheet. When frozen, pack in a rigid freezer container. Cover and label. Freeze up to 1 month. Do not thaw before cooking.
To serve immediately or after refrigerating or freezing: Heat oil to 375F (190C) or until a 1-inch bread cube turns golden brown in 50 seconds. Deep-fry frozen cakes in hot oil about 8 minutes or until golden and heated through. If cooking immediately or after refrigerating, reduce cooking time. Serve with green vegetables or a salad. Makes 4 servings.

Open freeze foods such as fish cakes, meatballs or meat patties. Place unwrapped items to be frozen on a baking sheet. Freeze until firm. Place frozen items in plastic freezer bags or rigid freezer containers. The amount needed can be removed without thawing, because items will not be frozen together. Reseal and return remaining food to freezer.

Cold Poached Trout with Hazelnut Mayonnaise

4 (7-oz.) trout, cleaned
2 bay leaves
Parsley sprigs
Salt
Freshly ground pepper

Hazelnut Mayonnaise:
1 egg
1 cup ground hazelnuts or walnuts
1/4 cup wine vinegar
4 to 6 tablespoons water
Salt
Freshly ground white pepper

To serve:
Parsley sprigs
Cucumber balls or small cubes

Some people object to seeing heads on cooked fish. Remove heads before serving, if desired.

1. Preheat oven to 350F (175C).
2. Trim trout fins. Put trimmed trout into a large shallow baking dish or roasting pan large enough to hold fish in 1 layer.
3. Cover with boiling water. Add bay leaves, parsley, salt and pepper. Cover with foil; bake in preheated oven 10 minutes. Cool in cooking liquid. When cool, drain cooked trout, discarding liquid and herbs. Slit skin from head to tail along back and stomach; carefully remove skin. Cover skinned trout tightly; refrigerate up to 2 days. Do not freeze.
4. To make mayonnaise, in a blender, process egg, nuts, vinegar and 1/4 cup water. Blend until smooth, adding more water if too stiff. Season with salt and white pepper. Cover and refrigerate.
To serve immediately or after refrigerating: Arrange skinned, cooked trout on a platter. Garnish with parsley and cucumber. Serve with Hazelnut Mayonnaise. Makes 4 servings.

Left to right: Cold Poached Trout with Hazelnut Mayonnaise, Seafood Continental with Spiced Rice

Seafood Continental with Spiced Rice

2 tablespoons vegetable oil
2 garlic cloves, crushed
1 lb. tomatoes (3 or 4 small tomatoes), peeled, chopped
2 canned pimentos, drained, chopped
1/4 teaspoon dried leaf oregano
3 tablespoons white wine or water
8 oz. cod or other white-fish fillet, skinned, chopped
6 oz. deveined, peeled uncooked large shrimp
4 oz. deveined, peeled uncooked small shrimp

Spiced Rice:
1 tablespoon vegetable oil
6 cardamom pods
1 (3-inch) cinnamon stick
1 cup uncooked long-grain white rice
2-1/4 cups boiling water
Salt

1. Heat oil in a medium saucepan. Add garlic; sauté 1 minute. Stir in tomatoes, pimentos, oregano and wine or water. Cover; simmer 20 minutes.
2. Add fish and shrimp. Replace cover; cook 10 minutes longer. Cool 30 minutes. Refrigerate overnight, or freeze.
3. To make rice, heat oil in a medium saucepan. Stir in spices. Add rice, water and salt; bring to a boil. Simmer 15 minutes or until water is absorbed and rice is tender. Cool.
To freeze: Pack fish mixture and rice in separate rigid freezer containers. Cover and label. Freeze up to 1 month. Thaw frozen fish mixture and rice at room temperature until partially thawed. Do not thaw completely.
To serve immediately or after refrigerating or thawing: Fish and shrimp are completely cooked; be careful not to overcook when heating. Heat fish mixture in a saucepan over low heat; bring to a boil, stirring occasionally. In another saucepan, combine rice and 2 tablespoons water. Cover; heat until water has been absorbed. Remove spices. Serve hot fish mixture over hot rice. Makes 4 servings.

Cod Steaks with Nutty Cheese Topping

4 (1/2-inch-thick) cod steaks
1/4 cup butter or margarine, room temperature
1 cup shredded Cheddar cheese (4 oz.)
1/2 cup chopped peanuts
2 teaspoons milk

1. Preheat broiler. Grease a broiler pan.
2. Place cod steaks in greased broiler pan; broil 5 minutes per side.
3. In a medium bowl, blend remaining ingredients; spread 1/2 over each steak.
4. Broil 5 to 10 minutes longer or until cheese topping has browned. Cool 30 minutes. Refrigerate overnight, or freeze.
To freeze: Pack cooled fish into a rigid freezer container. Cover and label. Freeze up to 1 month. Do not thaw before heating.
To serve after refrigerating or freezing: Place frozen fish in a greased baking dish. Cover with foil; heat in a preheated 350F (175C) oven about 20 minutes or until heated through. Reduce cooking time for refrigerated fish. Place under broiler to brown top, if desired. Serve with baked tomatoes and mashed potatoes. Makes 4 servings.

Lamb Strudel

2 tablespoons butter or margarine
1 onion, finely chopped
1 lb. lean ground lamb
1/2 pint dairy sour cream (1 cup)
2 egg yolks
3/4 cup dry bread crumbs
2 tablespoons chopped fresh dill
Salt
Freshly ground pepper
4 filo leaves
1/4 cup butter or margarine, melted
1-1/2 cups tomato sauce, homemade or prepared

1. Melt butter or margarine in a medium skillet. Add onion; sauté until onion is transparent. Add ground lamb; sauté until no longer pink. Drain off fat; spoon lamb mixture into a large bowl.
2. In a medium bowl, beat sour cream and egg yolks until smooth. Stir in bread crumbs, dill, salt and pepper. Stir sour-cream mixture into lamb mixture.
3. Unfold filo leaves; place on a slightly damp towel. Cover with another damp towel. Remove 2 leaves; place on a dry towel, slightly overlapping. Brush with melted butter. Place remaining 2 leaves on top of buttered leaves; brush with melted butter.
4. Spoon lamb mixture 1/4 inch from 1 long edge of buttered filo leaves. Fold long narrow edge of dough up over meat mixture; fold in edges at short ends. Use towel to roll strudel over, jelly-roll style, until completely enclosed in dough. Brush seam with water; press to seal. Lift in towel; roll onto ungreased baking sheet, seam-side down. Brush with melted butter. Cover with plastic wrap; refrigerate until ready to bake.
To serve immediately or after refrigerating: Uncover strudel; bake in preheated 350 (175C) oven 20 to 25 minutes or until golden. Turn over; bake 20 minutes longer. Heat tomato sauce in a small saucepan; pour into a serving dish. Slice strudel; serve with sauce. Makes 6 to 8 servings.

Double Rack of Lamb

2 lamb rib roasts, 6 to 8 ribs each, oven ready
Stuffing:
1/3 cup dried apricots
Water
2 tablespoons butter
2 medium leeks, cut into rings
1/2 cup uncooked long-grain white rice
1-1/2 cups chicken stock
2 tablespoons pine nuts
1/4 cup raisins
Salt
Freshly ground pepper

Ask your butcher to prepare the lamb for you. If paper frills are unavailable, make foil frills.

1. Place the racks of lamb together to form an arch. Crisscross bones. Refrigerate overnight, or freeze.
2. To make stuffing, soak apricots in water 30 minutes. Drain apricots, discarding water; chop soaked apricots. Melt butter in a medium saucepan. Add leeks; sauté until barely softened. Stir in rice; sauté 1 minute.
3. Stir in stock; bring to a boil. Cover; cook about 15 minutes or until rice is tender and all liquid has been absorbed.
4. Stir in chopped apricots, pine nuts and raisins. Add salt and pepper to taste. Set aside to cool. Refrigerate overnight, or freeze.
To freeze: Spoon cooled stuffing into a rigid freezer container. Cover and label. Wrap rib-bone ends with plastic wrap or waxed paper. Wrap roast in foil; label. Freeze stuffing and roast up to 1 month. Thaw overnight in refrigerator.
To serve immediately or after refrigerating or thawing: Spoon stuffing into center of roast. Cover rib ends with foil. Season with salt and pepper. Roast in preheated 400F (205C) oven 40 minutes or until desired doneness. Place cutlet frills on ends of bones, if desired. Makes 6 to 8 servings.

Double Rack of Lamb

Pork-Chop Casserole

8 pork chops
1/2 teaspoon dried leaf oregano
2 large onions, thickly sliced
1 small red bell pepper, cut into strips
1 small green bell pepper, cut into strips
1 zucchini, sliced
4 large tomatoes, peeled, sliced
1 teaspoon sugar
Salt
Freshly ground black pepper
1 cup red wine

1. Remove and discard bones from chops. Shape deboned chops into rounds, securing each with a wooden pick or string.
2. Grease a deep freezer-to-oven casserole; sprinkle with oregano. Arrange onions, bell peppers, zucchini and tomatoes in layers in casserole. Sprinkle with sugar; add salt and pepper to taste. Pour wine over vegetables.
3. Arrange boned chops on vegetables. Cover; bake in preheated oven about 1 hour. Cool 30 minutes. Skim off excess fat. Refrigerate overnight, or freeze.
To freeze: Cover and label. Freeze up to 1 month. Thaw at room temperature 3 to 4 hours or overnight in refrigerator.
To serve immediately or after refrigerating or thawing: Discard any fat from top of casserole. Heat in a preheated 350F (175C) oven about 45 minutes or until hot. Serve with new potatoes and a green salad. Makes 4 servings.

Pork-Chop Casserole

The following three stuffings are unusual variations suitable for chicken or turkey. Each recipe makes enough stuffing for a 3-1/2- to 4-lb. chicken. Double recipes to make stuffing for a 10- to 12-lb. turkey. Do not stuff chicken or turkey before freezing. Freeze chicken or turkey separately; stuff after chicken or turkey and stuffing have thawed.

Bacon & Brazil-Nut Stuffing

3/4 cup chopped cooked ham
1 small onion, finely chopped
2 cups fresh whole-wheat bread crumbs
2 tomatoes, peeled, chopped
1 Golden Delicious apple, peeled, grated
1/2 cup chopped Brazil nuts
2 tablespoons chopped fresh herbs
1 egg, beaten
Freshly ground pepper

1. In a medium bowl, combine all ingredients.
2. Refrigerate overnight, or freeze.
To freeze: Spoon stuffing into a rigid freezer container. Cover and label. Freeze up to 3 weeks. Thaw overnight in refrigerator.

Prune & Almond Stuffing

1 tablespoon butter or margarine
1 small onion, chopped
4 oz. lean ground pork
2/3 cup raisins, chopped
1 cup fresh bread crumbs
1/2 cup chopped blanched almonds
1 egg, beaten
Salt
Freshly ground pepper

1. Melt butter or margarine in a large skillet. Add onion and pork; sauté until pork is grey, stirring frequently. Drain off and discard fat. Stir in remaining ingredients. Cool.
2. Refrigerate overnight, or freeze.
To freeze: Spoon stuffing into a rigid freezer container. Cover and label. Freeze up to 3 weeks. Thaw overnight in refrigerator.

Cranberry & Rice Stuffing

2 tablespoons butter or margarine
4 green onions, thinly sliced
1 chicken or turkey liver, chopped
2 celery stalks, thinly sliced
2/3 cup cooked long-grain white rice
3 tablespoons cranberry sauce
1 egg, beaten
Salt
Freshly ground pepper

1. Melt butter or margarine in a large skillet. Add onions, liver and celery; sauté 5 minutes. Stir in remaining ingredients. Cool 30 minutes.
2. Refrigerate overnight, or freeze.
To freeze: Spoon stuffing into a rigid freezer container. Cover and label. Freeze up to 3 weeks. Thaw overnight in refrigerator.

If stuffing is baked separately, it is usually called a dressing. Dressing requires less time to cook and may be more practical when cooking for a crowd. Any recipe for stuffing can be used for dressing.

About 3/4 cup of stuffing is needed for each pound of ready-to-cook chicken or turkey. A Cornish hen will hold about 1 cup of stuffing. Allow room for expansion as the stuffing absorbs juices during cooking. Stuffing can also be used for fish and roasts.

Since bacteria grows rapidly in stuffing, there are safety tips that should be followed. Do not stuff poultry before freezing. Thaw frozen poultry before stuffing and cooking. Frozen stuffed turkey is available commercially, but commercial freezers freeze food more rapidly than home freezers can. Cook commercially prepared frozen-stuffed poultry according to package directions. Poultry should be stuffed immediately before roasting. Stuffing should reach an internal temperature of 160F (70C) during cooking. Always remove and separately refrigerate any leftover stuffing from the cooked turkey or chicken. Do not allow cooked stuffing to remain at room temperature for more than an hour before refrigerating.

Roast Stuffed Chicken

1 (3- to 4-lb.) roasting chicken
Stuffing:
12 oz. lean ground pork
1 small onion, minced
3/4 cup fresh bread crumbs
2 eggs, beaten
1/2 teaspoon dried leaf tarragon
Salt
Freshly ground pepper
1/4 cup butter or margarine
8 oz. chicken livers, trimmed
To garnish:
Watercress

Remove all bones except leg and wing bones. Leave them in to give chicken its usual shape. Carving is so easy that your guests will be impressed. To carve, cut off legs and wings; slice across body through meat and stuffing.

1. With a sharp knife, cut along length of backbone through tail. Cutting close to bone, gradually ease away meat and skin from around body carcass, as shown below. When you reach joint connecting thigh bone and body, break it away from socket, leaving bones in leg. Repeat with wing joints.

2. Be careful not to slit skin over top of breast bone. When breast bone has been cut free, lift out body carcass. Lay chicken flat, skin-side down.

3. To make stuffing, in a medium bowl, combine pork, onion, bread crumbs, eggs, tarragon, salt and pepper.

4. Melt 2 tablespoons butter or margarine in a small skillet. Add livers: sauté gently 5 minutes. Set aside to cool. Coarsely chop cooled livers.

5. Spread 1/2 of pork mixture down center of chicken. Spread with chopped livers; cover livers with remaining pork mixture.

6. Bring cut edges of chicken together again; sew with needle and kitchen string to enclose stuffing completely. Shape chicken into its usual form; truss to hold legs and wings in place.

To freeze: Do not stuff chicken. Package and freeze boned chicken, chopped livers and stuffing separately. Freeze up to 3 weeks. Thaw frozen chicken, livers and stuffing overnight in refrigerator. Stuff, as directed above, immediately before roasting.

To serve after refrigerating or thawing: Place stuffed chicken in a roasting pan. Spread chicken with remaining 2 tablespoons butter or margarine; season with salt and pepper. Roast in preheated 350F (175C) oven 1-1/2 hours or until a thermometer inserted in stuffing registers 170F (75C) and juices run clear when chicken is pierced with a knife between breast and thigh. Carve by cutting off legs and wings, then slicing across body through stuffing and meat. Garnish with watercress. Makes 6 to 8 servings.

Left to right: Roast Stuffed Chicken, Anniversary Chicken Pastries

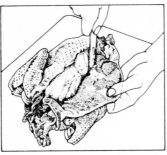

1/With a knife, separate meat from bone.

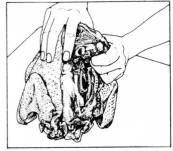

2/Break joint between thigh and body.

3/Cut breast bone free from meat.

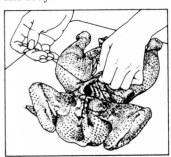

4/After stuffing, sew up chicken.

These are fun to make for a wedding anniversary or Valentine's Day dinner party.

1. To make pastry, in a medium bowl, combine flour and salt. Using a pastry blender or 2 knives, cut in butter or margarine and cream cheese until mixture resembles coarse crumbs. Sprinkle with 6 tablespoons water; toss with a fork until dough sticks together. Add more water, if necessary. Refrigerate dough 1 hour.

2. To make filling, melt butter or margarine in a large skillet. Add chicken; sauté 4 to 5 minutes or until lightly browned on both sides. Set aside to cool. In a medium bowl, combine almonds. cranberry sauce and onion. Season with salt and pepper.

3. To complete, cut chilled dough into 4 equal pieces. Roll out each dough piece on a lightly floured surface into a 9" x 8" rectangle.

4. Cut 1 dough rectangle in half crosswise. Lay a cooked chicken breast in center of 1 half. Spread chicken with 2 tablespoons cranberry mixture. Top with remaining dough half. Cut into a heart shape. Seal edges; crimp and flute. Place pastry heart on an ungreased baking sheet. Repeat with remaining dough, chicken and cranberry mixture, making 4 hearts.

5. Make decorative leaves or initials of anniversary guests with pastry trimmings. Moisten bottoms of decorations with water. Place decorations on pastry hearts. Refrigerate overnight, or freeze.

To freeze: Open freeze on baking sheets. When frozen, wrap in foil; label. Freeze up to 1 month. Thaw unwrapped pastry hearts on an ungreased baking sheet at room temperature 3 to 4 hours.

To serve after refrigerating or thawing: Brush with egg glaze. Bake in a preheated 425F (220C) oven 35 to 40 minutes or until golden brown. Serve hot. Makes 4 servings.

Anniversary Chicken Pastries

Pastry:
2-1/4 cups all-purpose flour
1 teaspoon salt
1/2 cup butter or margarine
1/2 (8-oz.) pkg. cream cheese, room temperature
6 to 8 tablespoons iced water
1 egg beaten with 1 tablespoon milk for glaze

Chicken Filling:
2 tablespoons butter or margarine, melted
4 boneless chicken-breast halves, skinned
5 tablespoons finely ground almonds
5 tablespoons cranberry sauce
1 tablespoon grated onion
Salt
Freshly ground white pepper

To *open freeze* means to freeze before wrapping. Place foods on a baking sheet or a plate, or freeze in pan or dish. This method is useful since many foods are difficult to package or wrap before freezing. Freezing firms the items and makes them more manageable.

Lamb Curry

2 tablespoons vegetable oil
1-1/2 lb. lamb stew cubes
1 medium onion, chopped
1 garlic clove, crushed
1 tablespoon ground coriander
2 teaspoons curry powder
1 teaspoon ground turmeric
1/2 teaspoon ground cumin
1/4 teaspoon chili powder
1/4 teaspoon ground cinnamon
1/4 teaspoon ground ginger
1/4 teaspoon freshly grated or ground nutmeg
1 tablespoon all-purpose flour
1 tablespoon tomato paste
1 teaspoon lemon juice
1 tablespoon shredded coconut
2 tablespoons raisins
1-1/2 cups hot chicken stock
Salt
Freshly ground pepper

1. Heat oil in a large skillet. Add lamb, onion and garlic. Sauté until browned. Stir in spices and flour until lamb is coated.

2. Stir in tomato paste, lemon juice, coconut, raisins and stock. Simmer about 30 minutes or until lamb is tender. Season with salt and pepper. Cool 30 minutes. Refrigerate overnight, or freeze.

To freeze: Spoon into a rigid freezer container. Cover and label. Freeze up to 1 month. Thaw overnight in refrigerator.

To serve after refrigerating or thawing: Heat curry in a medium saucepan; bring to a boil. Serve with hot cooked rice. Makes 4 servings.

Top to bottom: Lamb Curry, Moussaka

Moussaka

1 large eggplant, sliced
Salt
About 3 tablespoons olive oil
1 lb. ground lamb or beef
2 medium onions, thinly sliced
2 garlic cloves, crushed
3 tablespoons all-purpose flour
3 tablespoons tomato paste
1 teaspoon Italian seasoning
1/2 cup beef stock
Freshly ground pepper

Topping:
2 tablespoons butter or magarine
3 tablespoons all-purpose flour
1 teaspoon dry mustard
1 cup milk
1/2 cup shredded Cheddar cheese (2 oz.)
1 egg, beaten

1. Place eggplant slices in a colander; sprinkle with salt. Let stand 30 minutes. Rinse with cold water; drain.
2. Heat 2 tablespoons olive oil in a large skillet. Add drained eggplant slices, in batches; cook 3 minutes, turning once. Add more oil, if necessary. Using tongs, place cooked eggplant on paper towels to drain.
3. Add lamb or beef, onions and garlic to same skillet; sauté until meat is browned. Stir in flour until blended. Stir in tomato paste, Italian seasoning and stock. Cook until thickened, stirring constantly. Season with salt and pepper.
4. To make topping, melt butter or margarine in a medium saucepan. Stir in flour and mustard; cook 1 minute, stirring constantly. Stir in milk; cook until thickened. Remove from heat; stir in cheese until melted. Stir in egg.
5. In a large shallow casserole, alternate layers of meat mixture and cooked eggplant, beginning and ending with eggplant. Pour topping over last eggplant layer. Cool. Refrigerate overnight, or freeze.
To freeze: Cover casserole with foil; label. Freeze up to 1 month. Thaw overnight in refrigerator.
To serve immediately or after refrigerating or thawing: Bake in a preheated 350F (175C) oven 35 minutes or until hot and bubbly. Serve with a green salad and bread. Makes 4 servings.

Chicken with Apples & Cream

2 tablespoons butter or margarine
1 tablespoon vegetable oil
4 boneless chicken breasts, skinned
1 medium onion, finely chopped
2 Golden Delicious apples, peeled, sliced
1/2 cup apple juice
4 crisp-cooked bacon slices, crumbled
Salt
Freshly ground pepper

To serve:
2 Golden Delicious apples, cored, cut into rings
2 tablespoons brown sugar
1/4 cup butter or margarine
2 tablespoons Calvados or other brandy, warmed
1/2 cup whipping cream

1. Preheat oven to 375F (190C). Heat butter or margarine and oil in a flameproof casserole. Add chicken; sauté until browned.
2. With tongs, remove browned chicken from casserole; set aside. Add onion to casserole; sauté until softened. Add sliced apples, apple juice, bacon, salt and pepper.
3. Return chicken to casserole. Cover casserole; bake in preheated oven about 25 minutes or until chicken is tender. Cool 30 minutes. Refrigerate overnight, or freeze.
To freeze: Spoon sauce mixture into bottom of a rigid freezer container; add chicken breasts. Cover and label. Freeze up to 1 month. Thaw overnight in refrigerator or at room temperature 2 to 3 hours.
To serve immediately or after refrigerating or thawing: Place chicken, without sauce, in a baking dish; cover with foil. Heat in a preheated 350F (175C) oven about 20 minutes or until heated through. Meanwhile, coat apple rings in sugar. Melt butter or margarine in a large skillet. Add apple rings; sauté until browned. Remove from skillet; keep hot. Add sauce mixture to skillet; bring to a boil, stirring occasionally. Simmer until reduced by 1/3. Add Calvados or brandy; ignite. Shake pan until flames die. Stir in cream; adjust seasoning. Heat, but do not boil. Arrange hot chicken in a serving dish; top with sauce. Garnish with sautéed apple rings. Makes 4 servings.

Individual Beef Wellingtons

4 (6-oz.) beef-loin tenderloin steaks
Vegetable oil
1 garlic clove, crushed
4 oz. soft liver pâté
1 (17-1/4-oz.) pkg. frozen puff pastry, thawed
1 egg, beaten for glaze

---

1. Preheat broiler. Brush steaks with oil. Broil under preheated broiler 5 minutes per side. Cool.

2. In a small bowl, mash garlic into pâté.

3. Cut each pastry sheet in half crosswise. Roll out each half-sheet on a lightly floured surface into a rectangle large enough to enclose 1 steak.

4. Place 1 steak in center of each rectangle. Spread steaks with garlic-flavored pâté. Dampen edges of pastry; fold to enclose steaks. Press edges to seal. Decorate with pastry leaves cut from trimmings. Refrigerate overnight, or freeze.

To freeze: Open freeze on a baking sheet. When frozen, wrap in foil; label. Freeze up to 1 month. Thaw in refrigerator 4 to 6 hours.

To serve immediately or after refrigerating or thawing: Place unwrapped packets on a baking sheet; brush with beaten egg. Bake in preheated 425F (220C) oven 20 to 25 minutes or until crust is puffed and golden brown. Serve hot. Makes 4 servings.

Individual Beef Wellington

Beef Steaks Chasseur

1/4 cup butter or margarine
2 tablespoons vegetable oil
1 large onion, thinly sliced
1 lb. mushrooms, finely chopped
1/2 cup white wine
Salt
Freshly ground pepper

To serve:
6 (6-oz.) sirloin or porterhouse steaks, cut 1 inch thick
Parsley sprigs

1. Heat butter or margarine and oil in a medium skillet. Add onion; sauté until soft. Add mushrooms; sauté 8 to 10 minutes or until softened.
2. Stir in wine, salt and pepper. Cook 5 minutes longer; cool. Refrigerate overnight, or freeze.
To freeze: Spoon mushroom mixture into a rigid freezer container. Cover and label. Freeze up to 1 month. Thaw at room temperature 2 to 3 hours.
To serve immediately or after refrigerating or thawing: Preheat broiler or grill. Heat mushroom mixture in a medium saucepan until hot. Broil steaks to desired doneness. Place broiled steaks on individual plates; top with hot mushroom mixture. Garnish with parsley. Makes 6 servings.

Beef Steaks Chasseur

Beef & Ham Loaf

1-1/2 lb. lean ground beef
8 oz. ground cooked ham
1 large onion, minced
1-1/2 cups fresh whole-wheat bread crumbs
2 eggs
1 teaspoon dried mixed herbs, any combination
1 tablespoon chopped parsley
1 teaspoon salt
Freshly ground pepper

Topping:
3 large tomatoes, peeled, chopped
1 (7-oz.) can pimentos, drained, chopped
1 medium onion, thinly sliced

---

1. Preheat oven to 350F (175C).
2. In a large bowl, combine beef, ham, minced onion, bread crumbs, eggs, mixed herbs, parsley, salt and pepper.
3. To make topping, combine tomatoes, pimentos and sliced onion in a medium saucepan. Simmer 10 minutes or until vegetables are barely tender, stirring occasionally.
4. Spread topping in bottom of a 9" x 5" non-stick loaf pan or use a generously greased loaf pan. Spoon meat mixture over topping, spreading evenly. Cover with waxed paper and foil.
5. Place pan in a roasting pan containing about 1 inch water. Bake in preheated oven 1-1/2 hours. Remove waxed paper and foil. Cool 30 minutes. Refrigerate overnight, or freeze.
To freeze: Cover with fresh foil; label. Freeze up to 1 month. Thaw overnight in refrigerator.
To serve after refrigerating or thawing: Place covered loaf pan in a roasting pan containing water. Heat in a pre-heated 350F (175C) oven about 1 hour. Invert on a platter; remove pan. Serve with scalloped potatoes and green vegetables. To serve cold, line a platter with lettuce leaves; invert cold loaf onto lined platter. Makes 6 servings.

Variation
Pâté en Croûte: Do not make topping. Make pastry for a 9-inch double-crust pie. Line loaf pan with 2/3 of pastry. Fill with meat mixture; cover with remaining pastry. Brush with beaten egg. Bake in a preheated 400F (205C) oven 30 minutes. Reduce heat to 325F (165C); bake 45 minutes longer. Cool 30 minutes. Wrap as above; freeze. Thaw overnight in refrigerator. Serve warm or cold with a tomato sauce.

Roast Beef with Ale Sauce

1 (2-1/2-lb.) beef bottom-round roast
Salt
Freshly ground pepper
3 tablespoons all-purpose flour
1 cup light ale or beer
1 tablespoon tomato paste

To serve:
2 tablespoons butter or margarine
2 large leeks, cut into 1/2-inch rings
3 celery stalks, sliced

To garnish:
Celery leaves

---

1. Preheat oven to 325F (165C).
2. Place roast on a rack in a roasting pan. Season with salt and pepper.
3. Roast in preheated oven 1 to 1-1/2 hours for medium done, 160F (70C) internal temperature, or to desired degree of doneness.
4. Remove roast from pan; set aside. Spoon off excess fat from pan drippings. In a small bowl, blend flour and 1/4 cup ale or beer into a paste. Add remaining ale or beer to roasting pan; bring to a boil, scraping up browned bits for sauce. Stir in tomato paste and flour paste. Cook sauce until thickened, stirring constantly. Set aside to cool. Slice roast. Refrigerate overnight, or freeze.
To freeze: Pack roast slices in a rigid freezer container. Cover and label. Freeze up to 2 months. Pour sauce into a separate rigid freezer container. Cover and label. Freeze up to 2 months. Thaw frozen meat and sauce overnight in refrigerator.
To serve immediately or after refrigerating or thawing: Place meat in a shallow casserole. Cover; heat in a preheated 325F (165C) oven 20 minutes or until heated through. While meat is heating, melt butter or margarine in a large skillet. Add leeks and celery; sauté until softened. Heat sauce in a medium saucepan; bring to a boil, stirring occasionally. Pour hot sauce over hot meat. Serve with sautéed leeks and celery. Garnish with celery leaves. Makes 6 to 8 servings.

Variation
If desired, freeze meat and sauce in the same container. To serve, thaw and heat together in a medium saucepan over low heat.

Top to bottom: Beef & Ham Loaf, Roast Beef with Ale Sauce

Pork Strips with Sage

2 cups fresh white bread crumbs
4 teaspoons rubbed sage
1 teaspoon salt
Freshly ground pepper
2 (10-oz.) pork-loin tenderloins
2 eggs, beaten
Vegetable oil for deep-frying
Applesauce

Serve these for a dinner party with scalloped potatoes and broccoli.

1. In a shallow bowl, combine bread crumbs, sage, salt and pepper.
2. Cut pork into 1/4-inch slices. Cut each slice in half lengthwise to make strips.
3. Dip pork strips into eggs; coat evenly in crumb mixture. Place coated strips in a single layer on a baking sheet. Refrigerate overnight, or freeze.
To freeze: Open freeze on a baking sheet. When frozen, pack in a freezer container or plastic freezer bag. Cover and label. Freeze up to 1 month. Do not thaw.
To serve immediately or after refrigerating or freezing: In a deep saucepan or deep-fryer, heat oil to 375F (190C) or until a 1-inch bread cube turns golden brown in 50 seconds. Deep-fry frozen pork strips 5 to 8 minutes or until browned, crisp and cooked through. Reduce cooking time for unfrozen strips. Drain on paper towels. Serve with applesauce. Makes 6 servings.

Left to right: Pork Strips with Sage, Pork with Orange & Onion Stuffing

Pork with Orange & Onion Stuffing

2 tablespoons butter or margarine
1 large onion, thinly sliced
Grated peel and sections of 2 large oranges
1/2 cup dry bread crumbs
Salt
Freshly ground pepper
1 (3-lb.) boneless pork loin
1 tablespoon brown sugar

To garnish:
Orange slices
Lettuce leaves
Watercress

1. Preheat oven to 350F (175C).
2. To make stuffing, melt butter or margarine in a large skillet. Add onion; sauté until lightly browned. Stir in orange peel and orange sections, bread crumbs, salt and pepper.
3. Lay pork flat; spread with stuffing. Roll up to enclose stuffing; tie with kitchen string.
4. Place stuffed roast on a rack in a roasting pan. Rub with sugar, salt and pepper.
5. Roast in preheated oven 1-1/2 to 2 hours or until a thermometer inserted into center of stuffing registers 170F (75C). Juices should run clear when meat is pierced. Cool 30 minutes. Refrigerate overnight, or freeze.
To freeze: Wrap in plastic wrap and foil, or put into a freezer container; label. Freeze up to 1 month. Thaw in refrigerator 12 hours.
To serve immediately or after refrigerating or thawing: To serve cold, slice meat; arrange on a serving dish. Garnish with sliced oranges, lettuce leaves and watercress. Serve with a salad or pickles and hot baked potatoes. To serve hot, place in a roasting pan. Heat in a preheated 350F (175C) oven about 45 minutes. If desired, make a gravy from pan juices and 2 to 3 tablespoons fresh orange juice. Garnish as for serving cold. Makes 6 to 8 servings.

Deviled Pork Chops

6 large pork chops
Salt
Freshly ground pepper
1 (8-oz.) can tomatoes
3 tablespoons ketchup
1 tablespoon soy sauce
2 tablespoons Worcestershire sauce
2 teaspoons prepared brown mustard
2 tablespoons wine vinegar
1 tablespoon brown sugar

Hot cooked rice is a good accompaniment to this spicy dish. Double the recipe, if desired.

1. Preheat broiler.
2. Place chops on a broiler-pan rack. Sprinkle with salt and pepper. Broil until browned on both sides, about 10 minutes per side. Cool 30 minutes.
3. In a blender or food processor fitted with a steel blade, puree tomatoes with their juice. Stir in ketchup, soy sauce, Worcestershire sauce, mustard, vinegar and brown sugar.
To freeze: Place cooled chops in a rigid freezer container; pour tomato mixture over chops. Cover and label. Freeze up to 1 month. Thaw at room temperature 3 to 4 hours.
To serve immediately or after refrigerating or thawing: Place chops and sauce in an ovenproof serving dish. Cover; cook in a preheated 350F (175C) oven about 45 minutes or until heated through and bubbling. Makes 6 servings.

Variation
Omit tomato mixture. In a medium saucepan, combine 1 cup unsweetened apple juice, 3 tablespoons red-currant jelly and 1/2 teaspoon rubbed sage. Heat until jelly dissolves. Simmer 2 to 3 minutes to thicken sauce slightly. Pour over cooked chops. Freeze and serve as above.

Veal Marsala

2 tablespoons all-purpose flour
Salt
Freshly ground white pepper
Grated peel of 1 small orange
4 veal cutlets, beaten until thin
5 tablespoons butter or margarine
1 tablespoon vegetable oil
8 oz. button mushrooms, thinly sliced

To serve:
1/2 cup Marsala
1/2 cup dairy sour cream
Milk
Cooked zucchini strips, if desired

Turkey cutlets are a good substitute for veal. Substitute sweet sherry for Marsala, if desired.

1. In a shallow bowl, combine flour, salt, white pepper and orange peel. Coat cutlets with seasoned flour.
2. Heat 1/4 cup butter or margarine with oil in a large skillet. Add coated cutlets; sauté over low heat about 4 minutes on each side.
3. Remove cooked cutlets from skillet; set aside to cool. Add remaining tablespoon butter or margarine to skillet. Add mushrooms; sauté 3 minutes, turning gently. Cool. Refrigerate overnight, or freeze.
To freeze: Place cooled cutlets into a rigid freezer container. Add cooled mushrooms. Cover and label. Freeze up to 1 month. Thaw at room temperature 2 to 3 hours.
To serve immediately or after refrigerating or thawing: Place cutlets and mushrooms into an ovenproof serving dish. Add Marsala. Cover; bake in a preheated 350F (175C) oven 25 to 30 minutes or until heated through. Thin sour cream with a little milk, if necessary; spoon over heated cutlets. Serve with zucchini, if desired. Makes 4 servings.

Variation
Veal Grand Marnier: Substitute 2 teaspoons dried leaf tarragon for orange peel in step 1. Grate peel from 2 large oranges. Juice 1 orange; section other orange. Cook cutlets as in step 2. In step 3, omit mushrooms. Add remaining butter or margarine, grated orange peel and orange juice; bring to a boil. Add orange sections and 2 tablespoons Grand Marnier. Bring back to a boil. Serve cooked cutlets topped with a spoonful of orange sauce.

Ham & Cheese Pie

Pastry:
3 cups all-purpose flour
1 teaspoon salt
1 cup vegetable shortening
1 egg yolk
1/2 cup iced water

Filling:
16 oz. small-curd cottage cheese or
　ricotta cheese (2 cups)
2 eggs
1 teaspoon Italian seasoning
Salt
Freshly ground pepper
1-1/2 cups chopped cooked ham
1 (10-oz.) pkg. frozen chopped spinach,
　thawed, well drained
1/2 cup grated Parmesan cheese (1-1/2 oz.)
1 egg yolk beaten with 1 tablespoon milk for glaze

---

1. Preheat oven to 375F (190C).
2. To prepare pastry, in a medium bowl, combine flour and salt. Using a pastry blender or 2 knives, cut in shortening until mixture resembles coarse crumbs. Blend egg yolk and water; sprinkle over flour mixture. Toss with a fork until mixture begins to stick together.
3. Gather pastry; shape into a ball. Divide pastry into 2 pieces, making 1 piece 2/3 of dough. Roll out larger piece of pastry to a 14-inch circle on a lightly floured surface. Line an 8-inch springform pan with pastry. Press onto bottom and up side of pan. Do not trim pastry edge.
4. To make filling, in a blender or food processor fitted with a steel blade, process cottage cheese or ricotta cheese, eggs, Italian seasoning, salt and pepper until smooth. Stir in 3/4 cup ham.
5. Spoon filling into bottom of pastry-lined pan. Scatter spinach over filling; sprinkle with 1/4 cup Parmesan cheese. Top with remaining ham and Parmesan cheese. Brush edge of pastry with water.
6. Roll out remaining pastry to a 9-inch circle on a lightly floured surface. Place over filling. Crimp and flute pastry edges to seal. Slash center of pastry for steam vent. Brush pastry with egg-yolk glaze.
7. Bake in preheated oven 1-1/2 hours or until top is golden brown. Cool completely in pan on a wire rack. Refrigerate overnight, or freeze.
To freeze: Open freeze in pan. When frozen, remove pie from pan. Wrap in foil; label. Freeze up to 1 month. Thaw wrapped pie at room temperature 2 to 3 hours or in refrigerator overnight.
To serve after refrigerating or thawing: If desired, place on a baking sheet; heat in preheated 300F (150C) oven 20 to 30 minutes or until warm. Serve warm or cold with a tossed green salad. Makes 4 to 6 servings.

Clockwise from upper left: Brandied Chicken Livers & Noodles, Ham & Cheese Pie, Veal Marsala

Brandied Chicken Livers & Noodles

1/2 cup butter or margarine
1 shallot, finely chopped
1 lb. chicken livers, trimmed, halved
4 oz. button mushrooms, quartered
Salt
Freshly ground pepper

To serve:
8 oz. egg noodles
2 tablespoons butter or margarine
6 tablespoons brandy, warmed
1/2 pint whipping cream (1 cup)

To garnish:
Chopped parsley

1. Melt butter or margarine in a large skillet. Add shallot; sauté until softened. Add livers; sauté 3 minutes or until livers are no longer pink in center.
2. Add mushrooms; sauté 5 minutes longer. Season with salt and pepper. Cool 30 minutes. Refrigerate overnight, or freeze.
To freeze: Spoon cooled liver mixture into a rigid freezer container. Cover and label. Freeze up to 1 month. Thaw at room temperature 3 to 4 hours.
To serve immediately or after refrigerating or thawing: Heat liver mixture in a medium saucepan; bring to a boil, stirring occasionally. Meanwhile, cook noodles according to package directions until tender. Drain cooked noodles; toss with butter or margarine. Pour warmed brandy over livers; ignite brandy. When flames die, add cream. Heat but do not boil. Adjust seasoning. Serve brandied livers over hot noodles. Sprinkle with parsley. Makes 4 servings.

Spanish Paella

4 pinches saffron threads or 1 teaspoon turmeric
1 qt. hot chicken stock (4 cups)
1/4 cup olive oil
8 oz. boneless chicken, cubed
4 oz. lean boneless pork, cubed
1 medium onion, chopped
1 garlic clove, crushed
2 tomatoes, peeled, quartered, seeded
1-3/4 cups uncooked long-grain white rice
2 teaspoons salt
Freshly ground pepper

To serve:
About 2 cups fresh mussels, well scrubbed
4 oz. deveined, peeled, cooked shrimp
1 red bell pepper, sliced
8 pimento-stuffed green olives, halved
4 oz. frozen peas
8 large cooked unpeeled shrimp
Lemon wedges

1/Remove transparent pen.

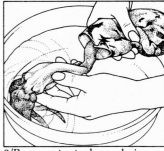

2/Remove tentacles and viscera.

3/Peel away speckled membrane.

4/Cut body into rings.

This traditional Spanish recipe is normally cooked and served in a paella pan. If desired, use a deep skillet with a tight-fitting lid for cooking; serve on a large platter. Double recipe, if desired.

1. If using saffron threads, soak in hot stock 5 minutes.
2. Heat olive oil in a large saucepan or deep skillet. Add chicken and pork; sauté until lightly browned. Add onion and garlic; sauté 5 minutes.
3. Stir in tomatoes and rice; cook 5 minutes. Strain stock, discarding saffron; add stock to pan. If using turmeric, add with stock. Cover with a lid or foil. Cook over a low heat 20 minutes or until rice is tender and liquid nearly absorbed, stirring occasionally. Season with salt and pepper. Cool 30 minutes. Refrigerate overnight, or freeze.

To freeze: Spoon cooled rice mixture into a rigid freezer container. Cover and label. Freeze up to 2 months. Thaw in refrigerator 12 hours.

To serve immediately or after refrigerating or thawing: Heat rice mixture in a large saucepan or deep skillet until hot, stirring occasionally. To prepare mussels, scrape off beards; discard any mussels that are open or broken. Steam cleaned mussels in 1 cup boiling water 5 minutes or until shells open, shaking pan occasionally. Discard any mussels that do not open. Keep hot. Add peeled shrimp, bell pepper, olives and peas to rice mixture. Cover; cook 5 minutes. Arrange cooked mussels, large shrimp and lemon wedges on top. Makes 4 servings.

Variation
Stir 12 ounces of cleaned squid, as shown above, in with rice and tomatoes in step 3.

Spanish Paella

Princess Sole

1 (15-oz.) can asparagus spears, drained
4 sole fillets (about 1-1/2 lb.), skinned
1 shallot, finely chopped
5 tablespoons dry white wine
5 tablespoons fish stock or clam juice
1/4 cup butter, cut in 6 pieces
1/2 cup whipping cream
Salt
Freshly ground pepper

If you ask, fish markets will often give you fish bones to make stock. Cover fish bones with water; add a little parsley, lemon peel, salt and pepper. Simmer about 15 minutes. Strain before using.

1. Preheat oven to 350F (175C). Grease a shallow baking dish.
2. Reserve 8 asparagus spears for garnish. Chop remaining spears.
3. Lay sole fillets, skinned-side up, on a board. Divide chopped asparagus among fillets; roll to enclose asparagus.
4. Sprinkle greased baking dish with shallot; arrange rolled fillets in dish. Pour over wine and fish stock or clam juice. Cover with foil; bake in preheated oven 10 minutes. Cool 30 minutes. Lay 2 reserved asparagus spears on each rolled fillet. Refrigerate overnight, or freeze.
To freeze: Wrap dish in foil; label. Freeze up to 2 months. Thaw wrapped fillets in refrigerator 6 to 8 hours.
To serve immediately or after refrigerating or thawing: Heat in a preheated 350F (175C) oven about 10 minutes. Drain liquid into a medium saucepan; boil to reduce liquid by 1/2. Beat in butter, a piece at a time. Beat until each piece is incorporated before adding more. Whip cream lightly; fold into sauce. Season with salt and pepper. Pour seasoned sauce over fish. Brown top of dish under a preheated broiler, if desired. Serve with mashed potatoes and green beans. Makes 4 servings.

Salmon Mousse

1 (15-1/2-oz.) can red sockeye salmon or pink salmon
1 (1/4-oz.) envelope unflavored gelatin
   (1 tablespoon)
1/4 cup cold water
1/2 (8-oz.) pkg. cream cheese, room temperature
2/3 cup mayonnaise
2/3 cup plain yogurt
2 tablespoons lemon juice
1/3 cup finely chopped dill pickle
1 teaspoon dried dill weed

For garnish:
1 hard-cooked egg
Thinly sliced pimento-stuffed olives
Chopped fresh parsley
Shredded lettuce leaves

1. Lightly oil an 8" x 4" loaf pan; set aside.
2. Drain salmon, reserving liquid in a 1-cup measuring cup. Add enough water to salmon liquid to measure 1/2 cup. Place salmon in a medium bowl. Remove and discard bones, if desired. Mash salmon with a fork; set aside.
3. In a small saucepan, combine gelatin and water. Stir well; let stand 3 minutes. Stir over low heat until gelatin dissolves. Add reserved salmon liquid; stir until blended. Set aside to cool.
4. In a medium bowl, beat cream cheese until smooth. Beat in mayonnaise and yogurt. Fold in mashed salmon, lemon juice, dill pickle, dill weed and cooled gelatin mixture. Spoon salmon mixture into oiled loaf pan; smooth top. Cover and refrigerate until set. Do not freeze.
To serve after refrigerating: Wet a clean dish towel with hot water; squeeze dry. Wrap hot wet towel around loaf pan 30 seconds. Invert mousse onto a serving plate; remove pan. Cut hard-cooked egg in half; remove yolk. Sieve yolk; finely chop egg white. Decorate top of mousse with rows of sliced olives, parsley, sieved egg yolk and chopped egg white. Surround with shredded lettuce leaves. Serve with a cucumber salad and boiled new potatoes. Makes 6 servings.

Seafood Salad

4 large scallops, fresh or frozen
1 bay leaf
4 (1-inch) lemon-peel strips
Salt
Freshly ground white pepper
3/4 cup cooked long-grain white rice
4 oz. deveined, peeled cooked shrimp
1 tablespoon chopped fresh parsley
1 tablespoon lemon juice
1/4 cup sliced almonds
2 celery stalks, thinly sliced
6 tablespoons thick mayonnaise
4 cleaned scallop shells

To serve:
1/4 cup mayonnaise
Cooked unpeeled shrimp
4 parsley sprigs
Paprika
Lettuce leaves, if desired

1. Place scallops in a saucepan with bay leaf, lemon peel, salt and white pepper. Cover with water. Simmer 5 minutes. Drain cooked scallops, discarding bay leaf and lemon peel. Chop cooked scallops; set aside to cool.
2. In a medium bowl, combine chopped scallops, rice, shrimp, chopped parsley, lemon juice, almonds, celery and mayonnaise. Season with salt and pepper. Chill before serving.

To serve: Spoon salad into scallop shells. Top each salad with mayonnaise, 1 whole shrimp, 1 parsley sprig and a little paprika. Garnish plate with lettuce, if desired. Serve with hot rolls. Makes 4 servings.

Left to right: Seafood Salad, Salmon Mousse

Desserts

Strawberry & Orange Gâteau

Cake:
3 eggs
1/2 cup granulated sugar
3/4 cup all-purpose flour
3/4 teaspoon baking powder
2 tablespoons hot water
Powdered sugar

Orange Butter Cream:
1/2 cup butter or margarine, room temperature
2 cups powdered sugar, sifted
2 tablespoons orange juice
2 tablespoons grated orange peel

To decorate:
1 cup sweetened whipped cream, page 71
1 pint strawberries, washed, hulled
1/4 cup red-currant jelly, melted

---

1. Preheat oven to 400F (205C). Grease an 11" x 7" baking pan. Line pan with waxed paper; grease paper.
2. To prepare cake, place eggs in top of a double boiler over hot water. Stir until warmed. Add granulated sugar; beat until mixture is thick and lemon-colored.
3. Pour egg mixture into a medium bowl; beat until mixture cools. Blend flour and baking powder; sift over egg mixture; fold in. Stir in hot water.
4. Pour batter into prepared pan; smooth top. Bake 12 to 15 minutes in preheated oven or until center springs back when lightly pressed. Sprinkle a clean dish towel with powdered sugar. Invert cake onto sugared towel; cool.
5. To prepare butter cream, beat butter or margarine in a medium bowl until fluffy. Beat in powdered sugar, orange juice and orange peel until fluffy. Set aside.
6. Remove paper from cake; trim crusty edges. Cut cake lengthwise into 4 equal strips. Spread top of each strip with butter cream. Roll 1 strip in a spiral, frosted-side in; lay, cut-side down, in center of a plate or baking sheet. Wrap remaining strips, frosted-sides in, around spiral, pressing strips against center of cake. Spread remaining butter cream over sides and top of cake.
To freeze: Open freeze cake. Wrap in foil. Label; freeze up to 1 month. Thaw unwrapped cake in refrigerator 2 hours.
To serve immediately or after refrigerating or thawing: Spread a thin layer of whipped cream around side of frosted cake. Spoon remaining whipped cream into a pastry bag fitted with a small rosette tip; refrigerate filled pastry bag. Arrange strawberries on top of cake; brush with melted jelly. Let stand until jelly sets. Pipe chilled whipped cream decoratively around strawberries. Refrigerate until ready to serve. Makes 6 servings.

Summer Lime Cheesecake

Crust:
1 cup graham-cracker crumbs
2 tablespoons sugar
3 tablespoons butter or margarine, melted

Filling:
1 (3-oz.) pkg. lime-flavored gelatin
3/4 cup boiling water
3/4 cup cold water
1 (8-oz.) pkg. cream cheese, room temperature
1/4 cup sugar
Grated peel and juice of 1 lime
1/2 cup whipping cream

To decorate:
1 cup sweetened whipped cream, page 71
Angelica leaves, if desired

---

1. To make crust, grease bottom only of a 9-inch flan pan with a removable bottom. In a small bowl, combine cracker crumbs, sugar and butter or margarine. Press crumbs onto bottom of prepared pan. Refrigerate until needed.
2. To make filling, in a small bowl, combine gelatin and boiling water. Stir until gelatin dissolves. Stir in cold water. Refrigerate until gelatin is slightly thickened and syrupy.
3. In a medium bowl, beat cream cheese and sugar until fluffy. Beat in lime peel and lime juice. Fold in partially set gelatin mixture until completely blended.
4. Whip cream until stiff peaks form; fold into gelatin mixture. Pour into crust; refrigerate until set.
To freeze: Open freeze chilled cheesecake. Pipe whipped cream rosettes onto an ungreased baking sheet; open freeze. Place whipped-cream rosettes in a rigid freezer container. Cover and label. Freeze up to 1 month. Wrap cheesecake in pan with plastic wrap or foil. Freeze up to 1 month. To thaw, unwrap cheesecake. Wet a clean towel with hot water; squeeze dry. Wrap hot towel around outside of pan; let stand 20 seconds. Remove pan ring; place cheesecake on a serving dish. Thaw in refrigerator 5 hours or until completely thawed.
To serve after refrigerating or thawing: Decorate chilled cheesecake with whipped-cream rosettes immediately before serving. Decorate rosettes with small pieces of angelica, if desired. Serve cold. Makes 6 servings.

Top to bottom: Strawberry & Orange Gâteau, Summer Lime Cheesecake

Oranges & Grapefruit with Caramel Sauce

4 large oranges, preferably navel
2 white grapefruit

Caramel Sauce:
3/4 cup sugar
2 cups water

---

1. With a small sharp knife or vegetable peeler, remove colored peel from oranges and grapefruit. Cut peel into thin strips; blanch in boiling water 1 minute. Drain.
2. With a sharp knife, cut white bitter pith from oranges and grapefruit. Cut fruit into slices or carefully remove each section. Refrigerate overnight, or freeze.
3. To make sauce, combine sugar and 1-1/2 cups water in a heavy saucepan over low heat. Heat gently, without stirring, until sugar dissolves. Boil rapidly until syrup turns a rich golden color.
4. Remove pan from heat; slowly add remaining water, a little at a time to avoid spattering. Stir until smooth. If lumps form, reheat and stir gently until lumps melt. Refrigerate overnight, or freeze.

Left to right: Oranges & Grapefruit with Caramel Sauce, Apple & Berry Pudding

To freeze: Put fruit, strips of blanched peel and sauce into separate rigid freezer containers. Cover and label. Freeze up to 2 months. Thaw frozen fruit in refrigerator 6 hours. Thaw frozen peel and sauce at room temperature.
To serve immediately or after refrigerating or thawing: Arrange fruit slices alternately in a shallow serving dish. Sprinkle with peel; pour a little sauce over top. Serve remaining sauce separately. Makes 4 servings.

Variation

Substitute tangerines, ugli fruit or red grapefruit for white grapefruit and oranges.

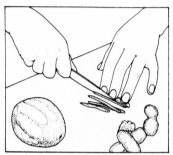 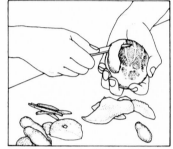

1/Cut orange peel into thin strips.

2/Remove white bitter pith.

Apple & Berry Pudding

3 tablespoons butter
2 cups peeled, cored, sliced cooking apples
2 cups blackberries, raspberries or blueberries
1/2 cup sugar
1 tablespoon tapioca
Grated peel of 1 lemon
1 egg, separated

To garnish:
1/2 cup whipping cream, lightly whipped

---

1. Melt butter in a medium saucepan. Add apples; cook over low heat until soft but not browned. Add berries; cook until tender.
2. Press fruit through a sieve. Return puree to saucepan; stir in sugar, tapioca and lemon peel. Beat in egg yolk; simmer 5 minutes or until thickened, stirring constantly. Cool. Refrigerate overnight, or freeze.
To freeze: Spoon cooled pudding into a rigid freezer container. Cover and label. Freeze up to 3 months. Package and freeze egg white separately. Thaw pudding and egg white in refrigerator 6 hours.
To serve after refrigerating or thawing: Spoon pudding into 6 serving dishes. Whisk egg white until stiff peaks form; fold into whipped cream. Spoon cream mixture on top of each pudding. Serve chilled. Makes 6 servings.

Chocolate & Chestnut Temptation

4 oz. semisweet chocolate
5 tablespoons butter or margarine, room temperature
1/4 cup sugar
7 to 8 oz. unsweetened chestnut puree (about 1 cup)
8 to 10 cookies broken into 1/2-inch pieces (2 oz.)
1/4 cup chopped candied cherries

This dessert is tempting without any decoration. For a special dinner party, decorate with piped rosettes of whipped cream and pieces of marron glacé.

1. Place chocolate in top of a double boiler. Stir over hot water until chocolate melts; cool melted chocolate slightly.
2. In a medium bowl, cream butter or margarine and sugar with an electric mixer until light and fluffy. Beat in cooled chocolate and chestnut puree until smooth. Fold in cookies and cherries.
3. Line a 7-inch springform pan with waxed paper. Pour in chocolate mixture; spread evenly. Make swirled patterns on top with a knife.
To freeze: Cover and label. Freeze up to 1 month.
To serve after freezing: Run a warmed knife around edge of frozen dessert to loosen it from pan. Remove ring. Invert dessert onto a plate; remove bottom of pan. Peel off waxed paper. Thaw in refrigerator about 1 hour before serving. Cut into wedges. Makes 6 servings.

Ginger Cream

1/2 cup whipping cream, whipped
1/2 pint plain yogurt (1 cup)
1/2 cup finely crushed gingersnaps
1 tablespoon candied ginger, chopped

To serve:
12 small candied-ginger pieces
Butter cookies

---

1. In a medium bowl, combine cream, yogurt and gingersnaps.
2. Fold in chopped candied ginger. Refrigerate.
To serve after refrigerating: Stir chilled mixture; spoon into 6 glass dishes. Top each serving with 2 candied-ginger pieces; serve with cookies. Makes 6 servings.

Whipped Cream

2 cups whipping cream
1 teaspoon vanilla extract
2 to 4 tablespoons powdered sugar

In a large bowl, whip cream until soft peaks form. Beat in vanilla and sugar to taste until stiff peaks form. Makes 3-1/2 cups.

Variations
To make **Chantilly Cream,** omit vanilla extract. Whipped cream can also be served unsweetened. If desired, substitute a fruit-flavored liqueur for vanilla extract.

Brandied-Fruits Ice Cream

1/4 cup dried apricots
Boiling water
3 tablespoons chopped maraschino cherries
3 tablespoons chopped raisins
3 tablespoons chopped mixed candied peel
3 tablespoons chopped green candied pineapple,
 if desired
1/4 cup sliced almonds
1 tablespoon maraschino-cherry syrup or
 maraschino liqueur
2 tablespoons brandy

Basic Ice-Cream Mixture:
2 eggs, separated
6 tablespoons sugar
1/2 cup whipping cream

This ice cream is very easy to make and does not need stirring during freezing. If desired, double basic recipe; divide in half and make two different flavors. Adding alcohol makes a softer ice cream so it can be scooped straight from the freezer. Thaw fruit-puree ice cream, below, in refrigerator about 1 hour before serving.

1. In a small bowl, soak apricots in boiling water 10 minutes. Drain, discarding water; chop soaked apricots.
2. In a medium bowl, combine all fruits and almonds. Stir in maraschino-cherry syrup or liqueur and brandy. Cover; let stand 6 hours, stirring occasionally.
3. To make basic ice cream, in a medium bowl, beat egg whites until soft peaks form. Gradually beat in sugar; continue beating until mixture is stiff and shiny.
4. In a large bowl, whip cream until thick. In a small bowl, slightly beat egg yolks. Fold beaten egg-white mixture and egg yolks into whipped cream until blended. Stir in soaked fruits and their liquid.
To freeze: Pack ice-cream mixture into a rigid freezer container. Cover and label. Freeze at least 6 hours. Store up to 2 weeks.
To serve after freezing: Scoop ice cream into individual serving dishes. Makes 4 to 6 servings.

Variations
Rum & Blueberry Ice Cream: In a medium saucepan, cook 2 cups blueberries and 6 tablespoons sugar over low heat until blueberries are tender, stirring frequently. Sieve cooked blueberries; cool. Stir blueberry puree and 3 tablespoons rum into basic ice-cream mixture. Freeze as above.
Mango Ice Cream: In a blender or food processor fitted with a steel blade, puree 12 ounces fresh or canned mangos. Add pureed mangos and 1/4 cup lemon juice to basic ice-cream mixture. Freeze as above.

Clockwise from upper left: Rum & Blueberry Ice Cream, Mango Ice Cream, Brandied-Fruits Ice Cream

Lemon & Meringue Torte

3 egg whites
3/4 cup plus 2 tablespoons sugar
Filling:
1/2 (14-oz.) can sweetened condensed milk
1/2 cup whipping cream
Finely grated peel and juice of 2 large lemons

To decorate:
Whipped cream
2 or 3 lemon slices, quartered
Chopped toasted hazelnuts or almonds

If desired, double filling, using whole can of sweetened condensed milk. Freeze half to use later in a trifle, to fill a baked pie shell or to serve as a pudding with whipped cream.

1. Preheat oven to 300F (150C).
2. In a large bowl, beat egg whites until soft peaks form. Beat in sugar in 3 batches; continue beating until mixture is stiff and shiny.
3. Line 2 baking sheets with parchment paper or lightly greased waxed paper; draw 3 (7-inch) circles on paper. Spread meringue evenly inside circles.
4. Bake in preheated oven 1 hour or until meringue is lightly colored and crisp. Leave in oven to cool. Peel meringue rounds off paper very carefully. Store tightly wrapped at room temperature up to 2 days or freeze.
5. To make filling, in a medium bowl, combine sweetened condensed milk, cream and lemon peel. Beat in lemon juice; continue beating until mixture is thick. Refrigerate or freeze.
To freeze: Pack meringues into a rigid freezer container with foil between each layer. Cover tightly; label. Pack filling into a separate rigid freezer container. Freeze up to 3 months. Thaw filling in refrigerator 6 hours. Separate meringues; thaw at room temperature on a flat surface.
To serve immediately or after thawing: Place 1 meringue on a serving plate. Spread with half of lemon filling; place another meringue on filling. Spread with remaining filling; top with last meringue. Decorate with whipped-cream rosettes, lemon quarters and hazelnuts or almonds. Serve chilled. Cut into wedges. Makes 4 to 6 servings.

Ice Cream Puffs with Hot Mocha Sauce

Choux Paste:
1/4 cup butter
1/2 cup water
1/2 cup all-purpose flour, sifted
2 eggs, beaten

To serve:
Hot Mocha Sauce:
2 tablespoons butter
2 tablespoons light corn syrup
2 tablespoons unsweetened cocoa powder
2 teaspoons instant coffee powder
3 tablespoons water
Ice cream for filling

---

1. Preheat oven to 400F (205C). Lightly grease a baking sheet.
2. To make pastry, heat butter and water in a medium saucepan until butter melts. Bring to a boil. Add flour all at once; beat until dough is smooth and pulls away from side of pan. Cool 3 minutes.
3. Beat in eggs, 1 at a time, beating well after each addition.
4. Spoon choux paste into a pastry bag fitted with a 1/2-inch plain tip. Pipe 8 cream puffs onto greased baking sheet. Or, use 2 spoons to make small mounds of dough.
5. Bake in preheated oven 25 minutes or until cream puffs are golden brown and firm. Make a small slit with a sharp pointed knife on 1 side of each cream puff; return to oven 5 minutes. Cool on a wire rack.
To freeze: Pack cooled cream puffs in a plastic freezer bag; label. Freeze up to 2 months. Thaw cream puffs at room temperature 30 minutes.
To serve immediately or after thawing: Fill each cream puff with ice cream; return to freezer. Make sauce just before serving. **To make sauce,** combine all ingredients in a small saucepan; heat until blended, stirring constantly. Boil 1 minute. Serve with filled cream puffs. Makes 8 servings.

Norwegian Apple Cake

1 cup sifted all-purpose flour
1 cup sugar
1 teaspoon baking powder
1 teaspoon ground cinnamon
1/4 teaspoon salt
1/4 cup vegetable shortening
1/4 cup milk
1 egg
1 teaspoon vanilla extract
1 cup peeled diced tart apple
1/4 cup chopped almonds
1/3 cup raisins

To serve:
Sweetened whipped cream, page 71, or ice cream

1. Preheat oven to 350F (175C). Grease and flour a round 9-inch cake pan.
2. In a large mixer bowl, beat flour, sugar, baking powder, cinnamon, salt, shortening, milk, egg and vanilla on low speed until blended. Increase speed to high; beat 2 minutes, scraping down side of bowl occasionally.
3. Fold in apple, nuts and raisins. Pour into prepared pan; smooth top.
4. Bake in preheated oven 40 to 50 minutes or until a wooden pick inserted in center comes out clean. Cool in pan on a wire rack 10 minutes. Remove from pan; cool completely on wire rack.
To freeze: Wrap in plastic wrap or foil; label. Freeze up to 2 months. Unwrap; thaw at room temperature.
To serve immediately or after thawing: If desired, heat in preheated 350F (175C) oven 10 to 15 minutes or until warm. Serve with sweetened whipped cream or ice cream. Makes 6 to 8 servings.

Clockwise from lower left: Norwegian Apple Cake, Lemon & Meringue Torte, Ice Cream Puffs with Hot Mocha Sauce

Fruity Bread Pudding

3 cups fresh bread crumbs
1/4 cup all-purpose flour
1/3 cup firmly packed light-brown sugar
1 teaspoon pumpkin-pie spice
1/4 cup butter or margarine, room temperature
1 egg, beaten
2/3 cup milk
1/2 cup dark raisins
1/3 cup golden raisins
2 tablespoons orange marmalade

1. Grease a 1-quart heatproof bowl.
2. In a medium bowl, combine bread crumbs, flour, brown sugar and pumpkin-pie spice. Add butter or margarine, egg and milk; stir until thoroughly combined. Stir in raisins and marmalade.
3. Spoon mixture into greased bowl; smooth top. Cover with a double thickness of greased waxed paper. Wrap with foil; secure with kitchen string. Cook immediately or freeze.
To freeze: Label. Freeze up to 1 month. Thaw wrapped pudding in refrigerator 6 hours.
To serve immediately or after thawing: Place bowl on a trivet in a large saucepan. Add enough boiling water to cover 3/4 of bowl. Cover; steam 2 hours, adding boiling water as necessary. Remove steamed pudding from saucepan; unwrap. Unmold pudding onto a serving plate. Serve warm. Pudding is delicious with custard sauce or ice cream. Makes 4 servings.

Clockwise from upper left: Fruity Bread Pudding, Custard Sauce, Pineapple & Cherry Steamed Pudding, Rhubarb-Ginger Sponge

Pineapple & Cherry Steamed Pudding

1 (8-oz.) can crushed pineapple, drained
1/2 cup butter or margarine, room temperature
1 cup sifted all-purpose flour
1/2 cup sugar
1 teaspoon baking powder
1/2 cup flaked coconut
1/3 cup chopped red candied cherries
2 eggs, beaten
2 tablespoons milk

To serve:
Sweetened whipped cream

1. Grease a 1-quart heatproof bowl.
2. In a medium bowl, combine pineapple, butter or margarine, flour, sugar, baking powder, coconut, cherries, eggs and milk; stir until well blended.
3. Spoon pineapple mixture into greased bowl; smooth top. Cover with a double thickness of greased waxed paper. Wrap in foil; secure with kitchen string. Cook immediately, or freeze.
To freeze: Label. Freeze up to 1 month. Thaw wrapped pudding in refrigerator 6 hours.
To serve immediately or after thawing: Place bowl on a trivet in a large saucepan. Add enough boiling water to cover 3/4 of bowl. Cover; steam 2 hours 15 minutes, adding boiling water as necessary. Remove steamed pudding from saucepan; unwrap. Unmold pudding onto a serving plate. Serve warm with sweetened whipped cream. Makes 4 servings.

Custard Sauce

1/4 cup sugar
2 tablespoons cornstarch
2 egg yolks, slightly beaten
1-3/4 cups milk
1 teaspoon vanilla extract

1. In the top of a double boiler, combine sugar and cornstarch. Whisk in egg yolks and milk. Place over, not in, boiling water.
2. Stirring constantly with a wooden spoon, cook 15 to 20 minutes or until custard coats a metal spoon and thickens slightly. Immediately pour into a medium bowl to cool. Stir in vanilla. Serve warm or refrigerate until chilled. Do not freeze. Makes about 2 cups.

Rhubarb-Ginger Sponge

2-1/2 cups fresh or frozen sliced rhubarb, thawed, drained if frozen
1/3 cup firmly packed light-brown sugar

Sponge Topping:
1/4 cup butter or margarine, room temperature
1 cup all-purpose flour, sifted
1/4 cup firmly packed light-brown sugar
1-1/2 teaspoons baking powder
1-1/2 teaspoons ground ginger
1 egg, beaten
1/3 cup milk

To serve:
Sweetened whipped cream, page 71

1. Preheat oven to 350F (175C). Grease a 9-inch pie pan.
2. Toss rhubarb with 1/3 cup brown sugar; spoon into greased pie pan.
3. To prepare sponge, place butter or margarine, flour, 1/4 cup brown sugar, baking powder, ginger, egg and milk in a large mixer bowl; beat at low speed until blended. Increase speed to high; beat 2 minutes. Spread batter evenly over rhubarb.
4. Bake 45 to 55 minutes or until a wooden pick inserted in center comes out clean. Cool completely in pan on a wire rack. Refrigerate overnight, or freeze.
To freeze: Open freeze. Wrap in foil; label. Freeze up to 2 months. Thaw wrapped sponge at room temperature 3 hours. Unwrap before heating.
To serve immediately or after refrigerating or thawing: Heat in preheated 325F (160C) oven 15 to 20 minutes or until warm. Serve warm with sweetened whipped cream. Makes 4 to 6 servings.

Variation
Substitute 2 tablespoons grated orange peel for ginger. Substitute orange juice for milk. Bake as above.

Honey-Apple Strudel

2 lb. tart apples, peeled, diced (about 6 apples)
1 teaspoon ground cinnamon
1/2 teaspoon ground nutmeg
1/2 cup chopped walnuts, pecans or almonds
1/3 cup honey
1/2 lb. filo dough (8 to 10 leaves)
1/2 cup butter or margarine, melted
1/2 cup fine dry bread crumbs

To serve:
Powdered sugar
Sweetened whipped cream, page 71

---

1. Preheat oven to 375F (190C). Grease a baking sheet.
2. In a medium bowl, toss apples, cinnamon, nutmeg and nuts. Stir in honey. Unfold filo leaves; place on a slightly damp towel. Cover with a second damp towel.
3. Remove 1 leaf; place on a dry towel. Brush with melted butter or margarine; sprinkle with 2 teaspoons bread crumbs. Place another leaf on top of first leaf; brush with butter or margarine. Sprinkle buttered leaf with bread crumbs. Repeat with remaining leaves.
4. Spoon apple filling on leaves about 3 inches from 1 long edge and about 1/4 inch from ends. Fold edges closest to filling over apples. Use towel to roll strudel, jelly-roll style, from folded long edge. Brush seam with water; press to seal.
5. Lift strudel in towel; roll onto greased baking sheet, seam-side down. Brush with melted butter.
6. Bake in preheated oven 30 to 35 minutes or until golden brown. Cool on baking sheet or a wire rack.
To freeze: Open freeze. Remove from baking sheet. Wrap in foil; label. Freeze up to 2 months. Thaw wrapped strudel at room temperature 2 hours. Unwrap before heating.
To serve later or after thawing: Heat in preheated 350F (175C) oven 15 to 20 minutes or until warm. Sift powdered sugar over warm strudel; cut into thick slices. Serve warm with sweetened whipped cream. Makes 8 to 10 servings.

Banana Puffs with Apricot Puree

1/2 (17-1/4-oz.) pkg. frozen puff pastry, thawed
2 large bananas
Vegetable oil for deep-frying
2/3 cup sugar
1 (8-oz.) can apricots, drained

Deep-fried puff pastry makes a delicious and different dessert. Cook puffs quickly in hot oil. Be cautious while frying; hot oil may spatter if pastry opens slightly during frying.

1. Roll out pastry dough to a 16-1/2" x 12-1/2" rectangle; trim edges. Cut dough into 16 (12" x 1") strips.
2. Peel bananas; cut in half lengthwise, then cut in half lengthwise again. Cut each piece crosswise, making 16 pieces.
3. Brush 1 strip of pastry with water. Place a piece of banana on damp pastry strip; wind strip around banana until completely enclosed, sealing ends well. Repeat with remaining pastry strips and banana pieces. Cook immediately, or freeze.
To freeze: Lay banana puffs on a baking sheet; open freeze until firm. Pack in a rigid freezer container. Cover and label. Freeze up to 2 weeks. Thaw banana puffs at room temperature 30 minutes.
To serve immediately or after refrigerating or thawing: In a large saucepan or deep-fryer, heat oil to 375F (190C) or until a 1-inch bread cube turns golden brown in 40 seconds. Add puffs to hot oil, 4 at a time. Deep-fry 1 to 2 minutes or until lightly golden. Drain on paper towels; sprinkle with sugar. Keep hot. Drain apricots, reserving syrup. In a blender or food processor fitted with a steel blade, puree apricots until smooth. Dilute puree with reserved syrup, if necessary. Serve pureed apricots as a sauce for hot banana puffs. Makes 16 puffs.

Variation
Pineapple Puffs: Substitute fresh pineapple for bananas. Cut unpeeled pineapple into slices. Peel slices; cut out center core. Cut each ring into 4 pieces. Wrap in pastry as above. Sprinkle pineapple puffs with sugar mixed with 1 teaspoon ground ginger. Serve with *Caramel Sauce*, page 70, if desired.

Shoofly Pie

Basic Pastry, page 27

Filling:
1/2 cup molasses
1/4 cup firmly packed dark-brown sugar
   or 1/4 cup honey
1/2 teaspoon baking soda
3/4 cup boiling water

Topping:
1-1/4 cups all-purpose flour
1/2 cup firmly packed light-brown sugar
1/4 cup butter or margarine

To serve:
Sweetened whipped cream, page 71

1. Preheat oven to 375F (190C).
2. Make Basic Pastry, page 27, through step 2. Roll out pastry on a lightly floured surface to 1/8-inch thick. Line a 9-inch pie pan with pastry; flute edge. (Do not prick pastry.)
3. To make filling, in a small bowl, combine molasses and dark-brown sugar or honey. Dissolve baking soda in boiling water; stir into molasses mixture.
4. Pour filling into pastry-lined pan.
5. To make topping, in a small bowl, combine flour and light-brown sugar. With a pastry blender or 2 knives, cut in butter or margarine until mixture resembles fine crumbs. Sprinkle crumbs over molasses filling.
6. Bake in preheated oven 30 to 35 minutes or until top is lightly browned. Cool completely on a wire rack. Refrigerate overnight, or freeze.
To freeze: Open freeze. Wrap in foil; label. Freeze up to 2 months. Thaw unwrapped pie in refrigerator 3 to 4 hours.
To serve after refrigerating or freezing: If desired, heat in a preheated 325F (160C) oven 15 to 20 minutes or until warm. Serve warm or cold with sweetened whipped cream. Makes 6 servings.

Clockwise from upper left: Honey-Apple Strudel, Shoofly Pie, Banana Puffs with Apricot Puree

Index